The
MIRACLES
of Jesus

VOLUME 2

CLARENCE SEXTON

CROWN
CHRISTIAN
PUBLICATIONS
Royal Reading

The MIRACLES of Jesus

VOLUME 2

CLARENCE SEXTON

FIRST EDITION
COPYRIGHT
MAY 2004

CROWN
CHRISTIAN
PUBLICATIONS
Royal Reading

PILLAR AND GROUND
OF THE TRUTH
CHURCH PLANTING AND
SUNDAY SCHOOL SERIES

THE MIRACLES OF JESUS
VOLUME 2

Copyright © 2004
Crown Christian Publications
Powell, Tennessee 37849
ISBN: 1-58981-224-7

Printed in the United States of America

Dedication

This volume is dedicated to the wonderful staff of Crown Christian Publications. They have faithfully labored to publish every book in this series.

Contents

Introduction

This introduction taken from *The Miracles of Jesus Volume I.*

THE MIRACLES OF JESUS

 very word in the Bible is written because God gave it. Every word of it is true, every word of it is holy, every word of it is profitable, and every word is eternal. The Bible says in II Timothy 3:16-17, *"All scripture is given by inspiration of God, and is profitable for doctrine, for reproof, for correction, for instruction in righteousness: that the man of God may be perfect, throughly furnished unto all good works."*

Our God is a miracle-working God. The Bible tells us in John 2:11, *"This beginning of miracles did Jesus in Cana of Galilee, and manifested forth his glory; and his disciples believed on him."* Note two extremely important words in this verse. The words are *"miracles"* and *"glory."* The miracles of the Lord Jesus manifested His glory.

Miracles are found throughout the Scriptures. The first miracle that the Lord Jesus performed was actually the miracle of creation. This miracle is recorded for us in the book of Genesis.

The Miracles of Jesus

The Word of God says in Genesis 1:1, *"In the beginning God created the heaven and the earth."* If you wonder who the Lord is speaking of in Genesis 1:1, consider Colossians 1:15-16. Speaking of Christ, the Bible says, *"Who is the image of the invisible God, the firstborn of every creature: for by him were all things created, that are in heaven, and that are in earth, visible and invisible, whether they be thrones, or dominions, or principalities, or powers: all things were created by him, and for him."*

> The miracles of the Lord Jesus manifested His glory.

Think of this, *"All things were created by him, and for him."* There are many miracles found in the Old Testament, but we are going to give our attention to the miracles of Jesus Christ recorded in the gospel records. These are the miracles we find in the Gospel according to Matthew, Mark, Luke, and John. There are about thirty-five different miracles of Christ given in the gospel records.

As we consider the subject of miracles, it will be most helpful to know what a miracle is. Many people call just about anything a miracle. Often the well-intended comments about miracles over-emphasize our ability and underestimate God's ability. But we can define a miracle as something that cannot be accomplished or explained merely by man's intellect or scientific effort. A miracle is not natural; it is supernatural. A miracle brings the supernatural into the realm of the natural. A miracle injects the supernatural with the natural order of things.

The Devil can also work miracles by supernatural power, but the miracles we are considering are the miracles of Christ. When we consider the miracles of Jesus Christ, we need to make note of certain things. *First,* we need to realize that they were performed in the presence of witnesses. This is important to remember. *Second,* these miracles

cannot be duplicated by scientific effort. Miracles cannot be repeated with man's effort, man's intellect, or some scientific achievement. A *third* thing we need to remember about these miracles is that they were given for a high and noble purpose, to help people and to glorify God. The miracles of our Lord Jesus Christ demonstrated His deity (Mark 2:7) and gave support to the fact that He is the promised Messiah (Matthew 9:27). Every miracle illustrates a deeper spiritual truth.

INVOLVING NATURE

As we consider these miracles, we will find that they involve nature. The Lord Jesus Christ spoke to a storm and said, *"Peace, be still."* In His first miracle recorded for us in John chapter two, He created wine from water. In His miracles, Christ demonstrated His power over nature. His disciples said in Mark 4:41, *"What manner of man is this, that even the wind and the sea obey him?"*

INVOLVING THE HUMAN BODY

We also find miracles regarding the human body. The lame were made whole. Withered hands were straightened. Blinded eyes were made to see. Miraculous works of God were performed on the human body. The Bible says in Matthew 11:4-5, *"Jesus answered and said unto them, Go and shew John again those things which ye do hear and see: the blind receive their sight, and the lame walk, the lepers are cleansed, and the deaf hear, the dead are raised up, and the poor have the gospel preached to them."*

INVOLVING DEMONS

There are also miracles concerning demons and demonic forces. People who were possessed with demons had them cast out as Christ proved His power over the Devil and his demons. We read in Mark 1:27, *"And they were all amazed, insomuch that they questioned* among themselves, saying, What thing is this? what new doctrine is this? for with authority commandeth he even the unclean spirits, and they do obey him."

INVOLVING THE MULTIPLICATION OF FOOD

Some of Christ's miracles involved the multiplication of food. The Lord Jesus took a little boy's lunch, multiplied it, and fed five thousand hungry men. The Bible says in Matthew 14:15-21,

> *And when it was evening, his disciples came to him, saying, This is a desert place, and the time is now past; send the multitude away, that they may go into the villages, and buy themselves victuals. But Jesus said unto them, They need not depart; give ye them to eat. And they say unto him, We have here but five loaves, and two fishes. He said, Bring them hither to me. And he commanded the multitude to sit down on the grass, and took the five loaves, and the two fishes, and looking up to heaven, he blessed, and brake, and gave the loaves to his disciples, and the disciples to the multitude. And they did all eat, and were filled: and they took up of the fragments that remained twelve baskets full. And they that had eaten were about five thousand men, beside women and children.*

INVOLVING THE RESTORATION OF LIFE

We also find miracles that have to do with the restoration of life. On three occasions, according to Scripture, the Lord Jesus brought a dead body back to life. Perhaps the most familiar of these accounts is found in John chapter eleven. Christ said, *"Lazarus, come forth"* (John 11:43), and Lazarus, who had been dead for four days, came forth out of the grave.

HIS BIRTH

Our Lord is a miracle-working God. Considering the Lord Jesus Christ, we believe that His birth was miraculous. No one was ever born like the Lord Jesus was born. He was born without the aid of a man. He was conceived by the Spirit of God and born of a virgin. A virgin brought forth what God sent forth. Christ did not begin in the manger; He did not begin with that virgin birth. He is coequal, coexistent, eternally existent with God the Father and God the Holy Spirit. His birth was a miracle.

Every miracle illustrates a deeper spiritual truth.

HIS LIFE

No one ever lived a life like Jesus Christ lived. He lived a sinless, perfect life. No one appeared in glory on this earth as Christ appeared when the Shekinah glory of God, the garment of deity, adorned Him on the Mount of Transfiguration. No man was transfigured miraculously as was Christ. His life was a miracle.

HIS DEATH AND RESURRECTION

No one ever died like Jesus Christ died. His death was a miraculous death because He dismissed His spirit. He was in charge of His own death. No one ever came forth from the grave, bodily, like Jesus Christ came forth alive forevermore. It was a miraculous death and a miraculous resurrection.

HIS ASCENSION

No one ever ascended as Jesus Christ ascended to heaven, defying all the laws of nature as He ascended upward to heaven. He was miraculous in His birth, miraculous in His life, miraculous in His transfiguration, miraculous in His death, miraculous in His resurrection, and miraculous in His ascension.

As Christians, we have a world view that the unbeliever does not have. When we consider our Savior and His miracles, we personally know a God who has done and can do the supernatural. It is one thing to talk about these miracles; it is another thing to place our faith in the God who worked these miracles. The true and living God, the God of the Bible, is a God of miracles. There are some simple things concerning His miracles that we need to know from Scripture.

THE PURPOSE OF THESE MIRACLES

The miracles of Christ are given to us with a purpose. Of course, we will consider what was done, but we must look beyond what was done and understand why these miracles were performed. They were performed with a purpose.

In John 5:36 the Bible says, *"But I have greater witness than that of John: for the works which the Father hath given me to finish, the same works that I do, bear witness of me, that the Father hath sent me."*

Note the expression, *"The same works that I do, bear witness of me, that the Father hath sent me."* The purpose in the miracles is to bear witness that Jesus Christ is God's Son, the Anointed of God, the Savior of the world. As we read our Bibles, believing what we find in the Bible to be the truth, let us look for this great purpose. The purpose is that people might believe that Jesus Christ is the Son of God, the Savior of the world.

THE POWER DISPLAYED IN THESE MIRACLES

In Luke chapter seven we read the story about John the Baptist inquiring of Christ. The Word of God says in Luke 7:19-22,

> *And John calling unto him two of his disciples sent them to Jesus, saying, Art thou he that should come? or look we for another? When the men were come unto him, they said, John Baptist hath sent us unto thee, saying, Art thou he that should come? or look we for another? And in that same hour he cured many of their infirmities and plagues, and of evil spirits; and unto many that were blind he gave sight. Then Jesus answering said unto them, Go your way, and tell John what things ye have seen and heard; how that the blind see, the lame walk, the lepers are cleansed, the deaf hear, the dead are raised, to the poor the gospel is preached.*

Take notice of the power of our miracle-working Savior. As we look at these miracles and see the Lord Jesus at work, our faith is increased. There is no one so far from God and so lost that God cannot change his or her life. We are to be witnesses to the miracles of changed lives.

THE PRINCIPLE OF THESE MIRACLES

The Bible says in Matthew 11:20-24,

> *Then began he to upbraid the cities wherein most of his mighty works were done, because they repented not: Woe unto thee, Chorazin! woe unto thee, Bethsaida! for if the mighty works, which were done in you, had been done in Tyre and Sidon, they would*

have repented long ago in sackcloth and ashes. But I say unto you, It shall be more tolerable for Tyre and Sidon at the day of judgment, than for you. And thou, Capernaum, which art exalted unto heaven, shalt be brought down to hell: for if the mighty works, which have been done in thee, had been done in Sodom, it would have remained until this day. But I say unto you, That it shall be more tolerable for the land of Sodom in the day of judgment, than for thee.

There is a principle found in these miracles. The Lord Jesus said in pronouncing this judgment that if the miraculous things that were done to those in Capernaum had been done in Sodom, Sodom would exist to this day.

> *The true and living God, the God of the Bible, is a God of miracles.*

The principle Christ declared was that God had privileged them to see something, to witness something, to be a part of something, and to fasten their eyes upon something that made them more accountable. God had allowed them to see the miracles that testified to His glory, His power, and His purpose. Because He had allowed them to see these miracles, there was a divine principle at work. They were more accountable than others because of the miracles they witnessed.

As we witness these miracles, one by one, studying them, talking about them, and gleaning from God's Word what God has for us in them, this same principle will be at work in our lives. What we know, what we witness, what we read in the Word of God, what we have experienced in our lives, and what God has done for us and for our churches makes us so much more accountable than others who do not know. We are more accountable than those who have never heard or those who have never experienced what we have experienced.

Even in the same church, there are those who are more accountable than others. No one knows exactly who those people are, but some people are more accountable because of what they have experienced in their walk with the Lord and what they have seen God do.

Every Christian should live a holy life and determine to walk closer to God. Let us love the Lord more for what we have seen and experienced in our own lives. How foolish it is to compare ourselves to other people when God has dealt individually with us. We have seen and known the power of God at work in our own lives. We are individually accountable to the Lord.

As we consider the miracles wrought by our Savior, there is a principle at work. God said it would not be as bad for Sodom as it would be for Capernaum in the Day of Judgment. The Bible says in Luke 12:48, *"For unto whomsoever much is given, of him shall be much required."*

The purpose in the miracles is to bear witness that Jesus Christ is God's Son, the Anointed of God, the Savior of the world.

As we think about our beloved America and what we have experienced in this country, the blessing of God has been poured out bountifully upon us. Think of what we have received from the mighty hand of God. God has singularly blessed our nation. This principle of accountability to God is certainly at work in the life of our nation. God will hold us in judgment in a way He will not hold other nations in judgment because of how He has blessed us. God will hold individuals among us accountable like He will not hold other individuals accountable. While we are thankful to God for the way He has blessed and worked in our lives, we must not forget our personal accountability to Him.

As we study the miracles of the Lord Jesus, remember that the purpose of these miracles is to bear witness that Jesus Christ is the Son of God. Remember also the power of our miracle-working Savior. He is still able to change lives today. And remember the principle that is always at work. As we witness the miracles of our Savior, we are accountable to Him.

Chapter One

WHAT ARE THEY AMONG SO MANY?

 he work of God is the work of multiplication. Once we truly understand this, our lives will never be the same. Our churches are to start churches that start churches that start churches. We train others to train others that they might train others. We bring people to Christ that they might bring others that bring others. Christ trained disciples to train disciples in order that they would do the same for others.

This miracle is about multiplication. It is mentioned in all four gospel records–the Gospel according to Matthew, the Gospel according to Mark, the Gospel according to Luke, and the Gospel according to John. In each account, a particular emphasis is made.

The record in John 6:1-14 says,

> *After these things Jesus went over the sea of Galilee, which is the sea of Tiberias. And a great multitude followed him, because they saw his*

miracles which he did on them that were diseased. And Jesus went up into a mountain, and there he sat with his disciples. And the passover, a feast of the Jews, was nigh. When Jesus then lifted up his eyes, and saw a great company come unto him, he saith unto Philip, Whence shall we buy bread, that these may eat? And this he said to prove him: for he himself knew what he would do. Philip answered him, Two hundred pennyworth of bread is not sufficient for them, that every one of them may take a little. One of his disciples, Andrew, Simon Peter's brother, saith unto him, There is a lad here, which hath five barley loaves, and two small fishes: but what are they among so many? And Jesus said, Make the men sit down. Now there was much grass in the place. So the men sat down, in number about five thousand. And Jesus took the loaves; and when he had given thanks, he distributed to the disciples, and the disciples to them that were set down; and likewise of the fishes as much as they would. When they were filled, he said unto his disciples, Gather up the fragments that remain, that nothing be lost. Therefore they gathered them together, and filled twelve baskets with the fragments of the five barley loaves, which remained over and above unto them that had eaten. Then those men, when they had seen the miracle that Jesus did, said, This is of a truth that prophet that should come into the world.

Typically, when this particular miracle is considered, much of the emphasis is given to the feeding of hungry people. However, when we talk about the work of God, feeding hungry people is a matter of great importance, but it is not the matter of most importance. Caring for the social well-being of human beings must always be a by-product of the gospel. It must not be the goal, but a by-product of the goal. If we make feeding and clothing people the goal of our ministry, we are far removed from what the Bible teaches.

New Testament missions is winning souls and establishing New Testament churches. New Testament missions is not going out and feeding the hungry, although feeding the hungry is a noble thing to do. Clothing the poor is a great thing to do, and I applaud the effort that people make in feeding hungry people and clothing people who are in need. However, we must not substitute that kind of work with the main work God has given us to do, which is leading people to Christ and establishing local New Testament churches.

In many parts of the world, there are people who are spending so much time and effort feeding the hungry, evidently without realizing that those hungry people are going to be hungry again; they will have to be fed again. The great tragedy is not that they will have to be fed again; the great tragedy is that if they could feed the hungry and keep them fed, they would still die without Christ and go to hell forever. The greatest thing we can ever do for someone is not to feed him with bread that fills his physical hunger, but feed him with the bread which comes from heaven, the Lord Jesus Christ. Only He can take care of his spiritual hunger. Of course, feeding him in his physical need gives us the opportunity to speak to him about his soul.

There are over six billion people in the world. I have read that one third of the world's population goes to bed hungry every night. I read in the same report that every day at least twelve thousand people starve to death in different places around the world. There is a tragedy in the deaths of these people, but there is also a tragedy in knowing that there is more than enough food in the world to feed the hungry. The problem is not with having enough food; the problem is not with the supply, but with the distribution of the supply. There is more than enough food to feed every hungry person on the face of the earth, but it is not being properly distributed.

We know from God's Word that the gospel is for all people. The Good News is that the Bread of heaven, Jesus Christ, came to earth and was born in Bethlehem's manger. He went to Calvary and tasted death for every man (Hebrews 2:9). He died for our sins. He was buried and rose from the grave alive forevermore. Jesus Christ will save all who come to Him by faith.

John 3:16 says, *"For God so loved the world, that he gave his only begotten Son, that whosoever believeth in him should not perish, but have everlasting life."*

You cannot tell the story of salvation to the wrong man. Everyone needs to hear that the Lord Jesus saves. He can save and will save all who come to Him by faith. The Bible says that He tasted death for every man. He shed His precious blood for a lost and dying world. Jesus Christ is powerful enough to save all who come to Him. The problem is not that there is not saving power; the problem is that the saving message is not getting out to the lost and dying. May God help us in the distribution of the Bread of heaven. Just as we need help in meeting the physical needs of the world, we need to concern ourselves with getting the spiritual bread to the spiritually hungry all around the world.

This is a beautiful story in John chapter six. There are so many spiritual lessons that God wants to teach us from this miracle.

THE COMPASSION OF CHRIST

In this miracle we see the compassion of Christ. When we read the four gospel records and frame this miracle in the context in which God gives it, we find that the disciples had been on a preaching mission. Two by two, they had been doing the work of the Lord. When they returned, they were tired, but they wanted to testify and talk about what God had been doing in their lives.

What Are They Among So Many?

When the Lord Jesus heard their reports, He said to them in Mark 6:31, *"Come ye yourselves apart into a desert place, and rest a while."* No doubt they were looking forward to that time of rest. They had been among the people, and the pull of the people had been upon them. They knew from observing Christ that there was hardly a waking moment when Christ did not have tremendous demands placed upon Him by the people.

Christ said to His disciples, "We are going to get alone, by ourselves, apart for a while and take a rest." The Bible says in one account that as they started out, and the multitude saw them moving, the people raced around the area of the Galilee in anticipation of where the Lord and His disciples were going. When Christ and His disciples arrived, a great multitude had already beaten them there. To the disappointment of the disciples, they saw this large crowd of people when they were supposed to have had their own private time with Christ.

The Bible says in Mark 6:34 that when the Lord saw the multitude, He *"was moved with compassion toward them, because they were as sheep not having a shepherd."* He suffered with them, not because they needed bread, not because they were hungry, but because they were as sheep without a shepherd. They had no direction, no purpose, no meaning, no shepherd. The Lord's heart was broken for them.

One of the things we have to deal with in our lives is the attitude these disciples developed about people. The disciples' attitude was, *"Send them away"* (Mark 6:36). They thought there were too many people, too much to deal with, and too many demands. This certainly was not the spirit of Christ.

Our feelings toward people are directly related to our fellowship with the Lord. When we do not have the right attitude toward someone, it is because we do not have the right fellowship with our God. If you are having trouble with someone, the real problem is not that person; the real problem is your fellowship with God.

There is a contradiction in life–the busier you get, the more you are involved, the more you are working, the more demands there are, it seems like the less time you have for the Lord. When the demand is great, that is when you need *more* time with God, not *less* time with God. We push the Lord Jesus aside until we finally get to the place where we are so ragged and so frustrated that we wonder if it is really worth it all. We are dying on the inside and active on the outside. Finally, God uses all that activity we have tried to substitute for spirituality to cause us to realize what the real problem is. The real problem is that we have forgotten the Lord. We are never going to be right about His work when we are not right with Him.

Christ's disciples needed to learn something–they needed to learn the spirit of Jesus Christ toward the people. The Lord had compassion on them. In any area of service in the church, any area in the ministry where you deal with people, if you are not careful, you will let people rob you of the blessing of serving God.

Let us be reminded here of the compassion of Christ. The Bible says He was *"moved with compassion."* He had compassion upon them.

THE COMMAND CHRIST GAVE TO HIS DISCIPLES

The second thing we must notice is the command Christ gave to His disciples. Let us look at two of the accounts. In John 6:1-5 the Bible says,

> *After these things Jesus went over the sea of Galilee, which is the sea of Tiberias. And a great multitude followed him, because they saw his miracles which he did on them that were diseased. And Jesus went up into a mountain, and there he sat with his disciples. And the passover, a feast of the Jews, was*

nigh. When Jesus then lifted up his eyes, and saw a great company come unto him, he saith unto Philip, Whence shall we buy bread, that these may eat?

Christ raised this problem to Philip. Let us not stop there. Verse six says, *"And this he said to prove him: for he himself knew what he would do."* Could it be that Christ created this problem in Philip's thinking to bring Philip eventually to a place of trusting Him?

In the record given to us in the Gospel according to Mark, the Bible says in Mark 6:32-36,

> *And they departed into a desert place by ship privately. And the people saw them departing, and many knew him, and ran afoot thither out of all cities, and outwent them, and came together unto him. And Jesus, when he came out, saw much people, and was moved with compassion toward them because they were as sheep not having a shepherd: and he began to teach them many things. And when the day was now far spent, his disciples came unto him, and said, This is a desert place and now the time is far passed: send them away, that they may go into the country round about, and into the villages, and buy themselves bread: for they have nothing to eat.*

In other words, the disciples were saying, "Get rid of them. Let's get rid of our problems by getting rid of the people."

Some people cannot get along with anyone, and their solution is to not have any ministry, not have any people, not try to do anything. They simply get rid of the problem by getting rid of the need.

These disciples said, "Run them off. Send them away." The Bible says in the record given in the Gospel according to Mark, *"He answered and said unto them, Give ye them to eat."* He commanded the disciples to feed them. Christ said, "We have five thousand men here, and you are going to feed them."

In John 6:5-7 God's Word says, *"He saith unto Philip, Whence shall we buy bread, that these may eat? And this he said to prove him: for he himself knew what he would do. Philip answered him, Two hundred pennyworth of bread is not sufficient for them, that every one of them may take a little."*

Can you imagine talking about *"a little"* in the presence of God Himself? Philip stood in the very presence of God, the Lord Jesus Christ–coequal, coexistent, eternally existent with God the Father, and God the Holy Spirit. He is God incarnate, Immanuel, eternal God. And Philip said, "Even if we spend everything we've got, we can't get enough to give everybody just a little." The Lord gave them something to do. There is no way these disciples could feed that multitude, but Christ said, *"Give ye them to eat."*

Our feelings toward people are directly related to our fellowship with the Lord.

God has given us a work to do–we are to preach the gospel to every creature. This cannot be done in our own strength. As a matter of fact, it cannot be done with our plans. He has given us a Book to tell us His plan. We can know His plan and still not get His work done because His plan and His work still do not get done without His power.

When I think about the needs of the world, I begin to tell God how needy the world is as if He does not know. I say, "Lord, do You know how many lost people there are? Do You know that there might be at least a third of the world's population that has never even heard about the Lord Jesus? Here is how we are going to tell them." God may let us use some ideas that we have, but He will not let us use them if that is what we come to Him with first and try to box Him in with our ideas. If we need revival of anything in the Lord's work today, it is revival of complete and total dependence upon God.

These disciples faced an impossibility that they were commanded to do something about. It is one thing to face an impossibility; it is another thing to be commanded by God to do something about it. This brought the disciples to a place of seeing their total inability and His complete and total ability.

COMING TO CHRIST

If we were the disciples, most of us would have said, "I'll tell you what we will do. We will make one great big pile of fish and bread and have everyone come and get in line. We will feed them one at a time. Everybody get in line, please." Can you imagine a line with five thousand men in it? We would have concocted some idea of dividing the group so as to not make anyone mad, dividing it equally and giving every man the same responsibility. But when we read the four gospel records, we find that the Lord Jesus did neither of these things. He blessed and broke the bread and distributed the lunch to the disciples.

> *We can know His plan and still not get His work done because His plan and His work still do not get done without His power.*

This whole miracle was designed so that the disciples had to depend upon the Lord. Christ had the disciples divide the people into groups of fifty and groups of one hundred. I would imagine that some of those men could handle groups of fifty and some of those men could handle groups of one hundred. The Lord knew who could handle the fifties and who could handle the hundreds. He knew what everyone was

29

capable of doing. We all will meet the Lord some day with our own ability and our own opportunity.

The race we are running is not against anyone else. I do not have to have a larger church than everyone else. I do not have to preach better sermons than anyone else. God expects one thing of me, and that is to do the best I can do with what He has given me. I must do my best with the ability He has blessed me with and the opportunity He has given me. This is all God expects from me and it is all God expects from you.

> *These disciples faced an impossibility that they were commanded to do something about. It is one thing to face an impossibility; it is another thing to be commanded by God to do something about it.*

The Lord Jesus blessed and broke the little boy's lunch. He commanded the people to sit down in groups of fifty and one hundred. The disciples came to Christ to get what they needed to feed the people. They started with just a few loaves and some fish, but every time they went to the Lord Jesus, there was enough to take care of their hundred or their fifty. There was not enough at the beginning for them to take care of five thousand, but when they made their trip to the Lord, there was enough to feed their fifty or their one hundred. He alone provides what we need as we need it.

God is never going to work in our lives where His work does not require faith. When those disciples made their way back to Christ, they had to believe that when they got there, He would have the bread and the fish for the hundred or the fifty they were commanded to feed. When they went back to Christ, they had to believe that He would have the bread and the fish they would need to go feed another hundred or another fifty. Do you know what we would find on that grass? We would find a well-worn path through the grass that led in one direction–straight to the Lord Jesus. There should be a well-worn path in our lives that leads straight to Christ.

When we think about our lives as Christians, I wonder how many of us would have to admit that the path of prayer does not really look much like a path because it is not worn. You may think sometimes, "Well, I know I should be closer to God." Do you know what brings you closer to God? You run to Him when you have to face an impossibility that you cannot handle.

Those disciples had gotten pretty disturbed about their private time being taken. Now they had been a part of this miracle, and they had seen the Lord Jesus do something magnificent. They knew that only God could do what He had done. Their faith had been strengthened. With a small boy's lunch, they had seen the Lord feed five thousand men. They had been a part of it because He used them to do it. Their lives were never the same because of it. When they looked back on that day, I am sure they were ashamed of how impatient they had been with the people because that was a part of what God used to bring them to Himself.

God expects one thing of me, and that is to do the best I can do with what He has given me.

When the people were dismissed, the Lord told the disciples to gather the fragments. John 6:13 says, *"Therefore they gathered them together, and filled twelve baskets with the fragments of the five barley loaves, which remained over and above unto them that had eaten."* They got the rest He had promised them after the miracle had been performed; they found a quiet place alone with God and had more than enough to eat.

Did you notice in this miracle that as long as there was a demand, there was a supply? There was more of a supply than there was a demand. The supply never exhausted when the demand increased. God's supply is never exhausted no matter how great the demand. You discover this great supply only as you reach the demand. As we demand, we find out something about His supply.

Do you think you would like to have been there that day to see God perform this miracle? Today, we have the same God. Christ said in John 6:35, *"I am the bread of life."* He can provide everything we need. If it is for fifty, a hundred, or a thousand, whatever we need today, He will provide. We must trust Him and seek Him for what we need to do His work.

*Chapter
Two*

WALKING ON
THE WATER

e do not hear it often today, but when I was growing up and people wanted to brag on someone to exaggerate what that person could do, they would say, "Some people think he can walk on water." We are going to consider the miracle of Christ walking on the water.

The Bible says in John 6:15-21,

When Jesus therefore perceived that they would come and take him by force, to make him a king, he departed again into a mountain himself alone. And when even was now come, his disciples went down unto the sea, and entered into a ship, and went over the sea toward Capernaum. And it was now dark, and Jesus was not come to them. And the sea arose by reason of a great wind that blew. So when they had rowed about five and twenty or thirty furlongs, they see Jesus walking on the sea, and drawing nigh unto the ship: and they were afraid. But he

35

saith unto them, It is I; be not afraid. Then they willingly received him into the ship: and immediately the ship was at the land whither they went.

In this passage, there are several things brought to our attention, but let us take the time to examine the same account in other gospel records. In the fourteenth chapter of Matthew, there are some things this writer, led by the Spirit of God, brings to our attention that we do not find in either of the accounts of Mark or John. The Bible says in Matthew 14:22-33,

And straightway Jesus constrained his disciples to get into a ship, and to go before him unto the other side, while he sent the multitudes away. And when he had sent the multitudes away, he went up into a mountain apart to pray: and when the evening was come, he was there alone. But the ship was now in the midst of the sea, tossed with waves: for the wind was contrary. And in the fourth watch of the night Jesus went unto them, walking on the sea. And when the disciples saw him walking on the sea, they were troubled, saying, It is a spirit; and they cried out for fear. But straightway Jesus spake unto them, saying, Be of good cheer; it is I; be not afraid. And Peter answered him and said, Lord, if it be thou, bid me come unto thee on the water. And he said, Come. And when Peter was come down out of the ship, he walked on the water, to go to Jesus. But when he saw the wind boisterous, he was afraid; and beginning to sink, he cried, saying, Lord, save me. And immediately Jesus stretched forth his hand, and caught him, and said unto him, O thou of little faith, wherefore didst thou doubt? And when they were come into the ship, the wind ceased. Then they that were in the ship came and worshipped him, saying, Of a truth thou art the Son of God.

Notice also the account found in Mark 6:45-52,

> *And straightway he constrained his disciples to get into the ship, and to go to the other side before unto Bethsaida, while he sent away the people. And when he had sent them away, he departed into a mountain to pray. And when even was come, the ship was in the midst of the sea, and he alone on the land. And he saw them toiling in rowing; for the wind was contrary unto them: and about the fourth watch of the night he cometh unto them, walking upon the sea, and would have passed by them. But when they saw him walking upon the sea, they supposed it had been a spirit, and cried out: for they all saw him, and were troubled. And immediately he talked with them, and saith unto them, Be of good cheer: it is I; be not afraid. And he went up unto them into the ship; and the wind ceased: and they were sore amazed in themselves beyond measure, and wondered. For they considered not the miracle of the loaves: for their heart was hardened.*

Notice what the Bible says in verse fifty-two, *"For they considered not the miracle of the loaves: for their heart was hardened."* I would like to begin with this fifty-second verse in Mark chapter six, where the Lord gives this footnote to this amazing miracle. I believe in doing so, He allows us to see that one miracle was not enough to keep the disciples going. They needed more than a miracle; they needed the Miracle Worker. They needed the Lord Jesus.

It is one thing to desire what Christ can do; it is an entirely different thing to desire Christ. It is so easy to spend time desiring what Christ can do or what He can give us. It is a great place in life when we go to the Lord absolutely empty and we say, "God, I just know I need You."

This is a rather strange statement God makes at the end of this story. In verse fifty-two of the account given in Mark chapter six, the Bible says, *"For they considered not the miracle of the loaves: for their heart was hardened."* The disciples had just seen Christ feed five thousand people. They had just had twelve baskets of food left over, one for each of them. That did not sustain them.

> *They needed more than a miracle; they needed the Miracle Worker. They needed the Lord Jesus.*

If you are living on some past experience, you are not living a victorious Christian life. We must trust God each day as if that were the only day we ever had to live the Christian life. There are things that build our faith; things that encourage us. There are things we remember that God did for us, but there is no victory in the Christian life living on past victories. We need the fresh touch of God daily.

In the record given in the Gospel according to John, we catch just a brief glimpse of Christ in the introduction of this miracle as the people wanted to make Him a king. That is not what He wanted. He did not want to be declared king because He met the physical needs of hungry people. He withdrew Himself from the multitudes and *"departed again into a mountain himself alone."* There He was in prayer, in that high mountain overlooking the Sea of Galilee. Then night fell.

THE STORM CAME

The Word of God says the disciples were in a ship crossing the sea. When a storm came, the Bible says that Christ had *"constrained"* them to get into the boat. *"Constrained"* is a powerful word. There was no room for debate when they heard Him speak about what they were to do. The Lord Jesus constrained them to get into the boat and go to the other side. He went to the mountain to pray.

As the disciples got into the boat and started to the other side, the wind suddenly became contrary; it was working against them. Sails were of no use; rowing was impossible. They were in the midst of a terrible storm. We find, by comparing the gospel records, that Christ did not come to their need until the fourth watch of the night.

Can you imagine how long they had been rowing in that storm? The Bible says that they rowed about twenty-five or thirty furlongs, which is estimated to be about half the distance across the sea. They were experienced sailors. They had been on that sea countless times, but now they feared for their lives. They were in the very heart of the Sea of Galilee, with the waves rolling and the wind blowing. They were terribly frightened, and in their thinking, Christ was somewhere far removed and out of sight.

Why did God allow this? Did He not care about them? Was He not able to do what needed to be done? There are so many times in life when we know God has put something in our hearts that we believe He is going to do. Faith must be exercised, not just to believe that God is going to do it, but to wait on God's timing to get it done. When the storm comes upon us, it is very hard to wait.

> *It is one thing to desire what Christ can do; it is an entirely different thing to desire Christ.*

The Word of God says in Isaiah 30:18, *"And therefore will the LORD wait, that he may be gracious unto you."* God knows when the timing is perfect. He knows in what watch of the night to come.

We are not going to live without storms. There is no painless way to follow Jesus Christ. Not every storm comes to us because of some sin we have committed. Many times there is suffering because of the sin of others. We must not try to play God and say to someone, "I know why this is happening to you." Leave it up to the Lord and His Holy Spirit to deal with people. But be assured of this one thing–the storms will come.

When the storm came to these disciples, Christ had constrained them. He had ordered them to get into the boat, and He had told them they were going to the other side. They were not going to perish in the midst of the sea. They were not going to lose their lives for one reason–Jesus Christ said that they were going to the other side. The sailing may get rough, but the harbor is always safe. He will bring us into our desired haven.

If you are living on some past experience, you are not living a victorious Christian life. We must trust God each day as if that were the only day we ever had to live the Christian life.

THE SAVIOR CAME

In the midst of the storm, the Savior came. He chose His time to come, and it was exactly what they needed. The Bible says they had rowed, and no doubt they were weary. It was the fourth watch of the night, and the peril had increased because of the darkness. They could not see Him.

On another occasion in Scripture, Christ was on the boat in a storm, and they woke Him. He rose and spoke to the sea and calmed the angry waves. However, this time He was nowhere in sight.

Even though they could not see Christ, He could see them. On that mountain where He prayed, He knew exactly what was going on. He knew what they were going through. He knew every emotion they were feeling. He knew every fear that filled their minds. He knew every wave that rolled against that boat. He knew every wind that blew against them. The Lord knew all about it; He saw it all.

In the fourth watch of the night, sometime between three o'clock and six o'clock in the morning, it was time to go to them. Christ went walking on the sea toward them. Can you imagine how fearful and how exhausted these disciples were? They had been out on the sea all the night, and then came the Lord Jesus walking on the water, and He made as if He would pass by them. They shouted, "Lord, we need You."

The Lord Jesus came tenderly, and they thought He was a ghost. He said, *"Be of good cheer: it is I; be not afraid."* Peter said, *"Lord, if it be thou, bid me come unto thee on the water."* Christ did not command Him; He invited him. He said, *"Come."*

Peter got out of the boat, put his feet on the water, and started walking on the water. The boisterous waves came rolling, and Peter took His eyes off Christ. He looked at the waves, and he started to sink. He immediately cried out, *"Lord, save me."* The Lord Jesus reached out with His hand, pulled him from the angry waves, and brought him safely on board.

You may think, "My storm has been going on a long time." Maybe you have already guessed what watch of the night you are in. God has not deserted His children. Just as surely as the storms come, the Savior will also come. Everything these disciples were frightened of was under His feet. Everything that scared them, He had conquered.

As we think about our Savior coming to us, what are we most thrilled with–His power or His love? Can we separate the two? What thrills my soul most is not that He can put the storm under His feet;

There are so many times in life when we know God has put something in our hearts that we believe He is going to do. Faith must be exercised, not just to believe that God is going to do it, but to wait on God's timing to get it done.

what thrills my soul most is that He loves me enough to come to my aid. Someone may say, "You cannot measure His power; He is an omnipotent God." I agree. We cannot measure His power. He is all-powerful. However, neither can you measure His love. He is all-loving.

The Devil plays the same trick on all of us. He likes to blind us to the goodness of God. Why? Because the Bible says in Romans 2:4, *"The goodness of God leadeth thee to repentance."* The Devil says, "If God really cared about you, He would not have allowed this to happen to you."

The Bible says in Romans 8:35-39,

> *Who shall separate us from the love of Christ? shall tribulation, or distress, or persecution, or famine, or nakedness, or peril, or sword? As it is written, For thy sake we are killed all the day long; we are accounted as sheep for the slaughter. Nay, in all these things we are more than conquerors through him that loved us. For I am persuaded, that neither death, nor life, nor angels, nor principalities, nor powers, nor things present, nor things to come, nor height, nor depth, nor any other creature, shall be able to separate us from the love of God, which is in Christ Jesus our Lord.*

In Ephesians 3:17-19 the Bible says,

> *That Christ may dwell in your hearts by faith; that ye, being rooted and grounded in love, may be able to comprehend with all saints what is the breadth, and length, and depth, and height; and to know the love of Christ, which passeth knowledge, that ye might be filled with all the fulness of God.*

In other words, God declares to us that as we think on His love, experience His love, and are captured by His love, it has a transforming effect on us with all the fullness of God. Verses twenty and twenty-one continue, *"Now unto him that is able to do exceeding abundantly above all that we ask or think, according to the power that worketh in us, unto him be glory in the church by Christ Jesus throughout all ages, world without end. Amen."*

At times, we wonder, "Lord, I know You are able to do this. You spoke the world into existence. Why don't You come and intervene?" Let us drive this a thousand miles deep into our souls—we must never doubt that God loves us. In His time, He will come to our aid,

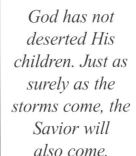

> *God has not deserted His children. Just as surely as the storms come, the Savior will also come.*

walking on the water with everything that troubles us under His feet. He was up in that high mountain praying. He is in a higher place now praying at the right hand of God the Father, ever living to make intercession for us. He will never leave us alone or forsake us.

THE STILLNESS CAME

In this miracle, we see that the storm came, the Savior came, and the stillness came. The wind was boisterous and contrary. The Word of God says Christ spoke to His disciples. In John 6:20-21 the Bible says, *"But he saith unto them, It is I; be not afraid. Then they willingly received him into the ship: and immediately the ship was at the land whither they went."*

I do not understand everything about that twenty-first verse, but I do find that when He came to them in the middle of the sea, immediately they were at their destination. I understand from this that when the Lord Jesus arrives, He is all we need.

Notice the calm, the stillness. The Bible says in Mark 6:51, *"And he went up unto them into the ship; and the wind ceased: and they were sore amazed in themselves beyond measure, and wondered."* They should not have been *"sore amazed...beyond measure"* because they had just seen Him feed five thousand men from one little boy's lunch.

The Bible says in Matthew 14:31-32,

> *And immediately Jesus stretched forth his hand, and caught him, and said unto him, O thou of little faith, wherefore didst thou doubt? And when they were come into the ship, the wind ceased. Then they that were in the ship came and worshipped him, saying, Of a truth thou art the Son of God.*

The storm came, the Savior came, and the stillness came. Not only was the storm stilled, their hearts were stilled. They had peace in the midst of the storm. There is a great lesson in this miracle. The lesson is that nothing is too great for Christ to conquer, and when He comes, all is well.

Christ knows what we need. He knew these disciples were going to make it to the other side, but He knew they needed a storm on the way over. He allowed the storm. He went to them in the fourth watch of the night in the midst of the sea, and He proved again to them that He is God.

Chapter Three

GREAT FAITH IN AN UNEXPECTED PLACE

"A WOMAN OF GREAT FAITH"

he miracles of Christ recorded for us in God's Word provide the opportunity for us to give serious thought to what the Lord can accomplish in our lives. Our God is the same yesterday, today, and forever. In this story, as far as we know, Christ traveled a great distance and stayed for only a brief period of time to work this miracle and bring this one woman to Himself. The Bible says in Matthew 15:21-28,

> *Then Jesus went thence, and departed into the coasts of Tyre and Sidon. And, behold, a woman of Canaan came out of the same coasts, and cried unto him, saying, Have mercy on me, O Lord, thou son of David; my daughter is grievously vexed with a devil. But he answered her not a word. And his disciples came and besought him, saying, Send*

her away; for she crieth after us. But he answered and said, I am not sent but unto the lost sheep of the house of Israel. Then came she and worshipped him, saying, Lord, help me. But he answered and said, It is not meet to take the children's bread, and cast it to dogs. And she said, Truth, Lord: yet the dogs eat of the crumbs which fall from their masters' table. Then Jesus answered and said unto her, O woman, great is thy faith: be it unto thee even as thou wilt. And her daughter was made whole from that very hour.

The Bible says in verse twenty-eight, *"O woman, great is thy faith."* Some people may have the mistaken idea that it takes a man to express great faith in God. Not only was this particular individual a woman, but the Bible says in Mark chapter seven that she was a Syrophenician woman.

Early in the fifteenth chapter of the Gospel according to Matthew, we find that the Lord Jesus was dealing with the Pharisees. The Bible says in verses one through four,

Then came to Jesus scribes and Pharisees, which were of Jerusalem, saying, Why do thy disciples transgress the tradition of the elders? for they wash not their hands when they eat bread. But he answered and said unto them, Why do ye also transgress the commandment of God by your tradition? For God commanded, saying, Honour thy father and mother: and, He that curseth father or mother, let him die the death.

Christ continued by explaining to the Pharisees what their sin was. Notice what the Word of God says in verses seven through eleven of Matthew chapter fifteen,

> *Ye hypocrites, well did Esaias prophesy of you, saying, This people draweth nigh unto me with their mouth, and honoureth me with their lips; but their heart is far from me. But in vain they do worship me, teaching for doctrines the commandments of men. And he called the multitude, and said unto them, Hear, and understand: not that which goeth into the mouth defileth a man; but that which cometh out of the mouth, this defileth a man.*

The Lord Jesus called the whole multitude together and said, "I want you to know about these Pharisees. They are hypocrites." The Word of God says in verse twelve, *"Then came his disciples, and said unto him, Knowest thou that the Pharisees were offended, after they heard this saying?"* The disciples said, "You made the Pharisees mad. You have offended them. Don't You know what You've done?"

The Lord Jesus answered their question, *"Every plant, which my heavenly Father hath not planted, shall be rooted up. Let them alone: they be blind leaders of the blind. And if the blind lead the blind, both shall fall into the ditch."* He said, "These are blind people. Leave them alone. The blind are leading the blind." The Lord Jesus knew full well what He had said to them.

In this story of the Syrophenician woman and her faith, the Word of God says that Christ left the area of the Jews. It is as though He grew weary of their hypocrisy. Excuse the expression, it is as though He "took a break" from these hypocrites.

The Word of God says in Matthew 15:21, *"Then Jesus went thence, and departed into the coasts of Tyre and Sidon."* When He went to deal with the Syrophenician woman, He was going to an area where one would not expect any good thing to take place. It is an area where one would never expect to find great faith in God, but He found something there that He did not find among the leaders of Judaism.

Most of the time, we have preconceived ideas about where God is going to work and about where we are going to find great faith in God. When we have these preconceived ideas, we are "soil sampling" before we do our "seed sowing." This is always a mistake. God did not call us to sample the soil, He called us to sow the seed. Wherever we go, we are to tell everyone that Christ is the only way to heaven. He knows where the fertile soil is found. We are to go, sow the seed, and leave everything else in God's hands.

> *God did not call us to sample the soil, He called us to sow the seed.*

A mighty miracle was about to take place along the coast of the Mediterranean Sea. The Bible says that Christ traveled to the cities of Tyre and Sidon. Syria had captured this Phoenician area, so the people were referred to as Syrophenicians. The woman He met was a Syrophenician.

This woman was also called a Canaanite. In the tenth chapter of the book of Genesis, we find that Noah had sons, and his sons had sons. In the lineage of Ham, we find a man by the name of Canaan. Canaan had a son whose name was Sidon, and they settled in this land that became known as the land of Canaan. Sidon settled along the Mediterranean Sea coast, and this very old city was called Sidon after the son of Canaan.

As the Lord Jesus traveled to this area of Tyre and Sidon in the land of the Syrophenicians, He came in contact with this Syrophenician woman. He wrought a mighty miracle in her life.

THE REQUEST OF THE SYROPHENICIAN WOMAN

Notice the request of the Syrophenician woman. The Bible says in verses twenty-one and twenty-two, *"Then Jesus went thence, and departed into the coasts of Tyre and Sidon. And, behold, a woman of Canaan came out of the same coasts, and cried unto him, saying, Have mercy on me, O Lord, thou Son of David."* Take note of the pronoun *"me."* She said, *"Have mercy on me."* She was asking help for her daughter, but she so identified herself with the need of her daughter that when she came to Christ, she said, *"Have mercy on me."* Three times she made this request. Notice what the Bible says,

> *But he answered her not a word. And his disciples came and besought him, saying, Send her away; for she crieth after us. But he answered and said, I am not sent but unto the lost sheep of the house of Israel. Then came she and worshipped him, saying, Lord, help me. But he answered and said, It is not meet to take the children's bread, and cast it to dogs. And she said, Truth, Lord: yet the dogs eat of the crumbs which fall from their masters' table.*

She said again and again, *"Lord, help me."* A third time, the woman made her request to the Lord Jesus Christ. What Christ said to her was amazing.

This mother was so greatly burdened that she went to Christ, so inseparably knit together with the need of her daughter, that she asked help for herself because her burden for her daughter was so great. Thinking as I read this, I did not ask myself if I had the love for my children to bring them to God, but if I had the faith in God to bring my children to Him.

Many are disturbed about the needs of their children. It is one thing to be troubled about your children's needs; it is another thing to believe that God and God alone can meet the needs of your children. It is one thing to get troubled about what is going wrong in your children's lives; it is another thing entirely to come to the place where you have such faith in God that you know only God can work out what is wrong in the lives of your children.

> *It is one thing to be troubled about your children's needs; it is another thing to believe that God and God alone can meet the needs of your children.*

This woman was so burdened for her daughter. More importantly, it was not her burden for her daughter, but her faith and belief in the Son of God that caused her to go to Jesus Christ. She had heard there was a Hebrew, one of the Jews, the Savior of the world, a healer of men who was able to do all things. When Christ Jesus came into the area where she lived, the Bible says she went out to meet Him and make known to Him the burden of her heart because she knew that only the Lord Jesus could meet that need. We spend so much time talking about our lives, and so little of our lives bringing our burdens to the Lord. She made her request known to the Lord Jesus. Think of how Christ was seeking this woman in her need.

THE RESPONSE OF THE LORD JESUS CHRIST

When we read this passage, we may at first be troubled by what Christ said. The Bible says in Matthew 15:21-23, *"Then Jesus went thence, and departed into the coasts of Tyre and Sidon. And, behold, a woman of Canaan came out of the same coasts, and cried unto him, saying, Have mercy on me, O Lord, thou Son of David; my daughter is grievously vexed with a devil. But he answered her not a word."*

When God is silent, it is not because He does not hear. There is a definite reason why He did not answer this woman at that time.

When Jesus Christ came into the world, He chose a certain way to do His work. He did not go to some great city and begin to lecture and try to influence people. He chose a small group of men and trained them. He knew He would go to Calvary to bleed and die for the sins of the whole world, tasting death for every man. He would shed His precious blood, die, be buried, and rise from the dead on the third day. He would ascend to heaven and leave His work in the hearts and hands of His disciples who would be empowered by the continuing Christ in the Person of the Holy Spirit. They had to learn from Him how His work was to be done. They had to learn to trust Him.

His disciples observed this entire matter. They were with Him when He declared the hypocrisy of the Pharisees. They were with Him at the conclusion of this miracle when they saw the mighty works that were done in response to the faith of this Syrophenician woman. They saw God do a greater work among the heathen than He could do among the religious traditionalists. They saw what it meant to find a fertile heart who would trust God, and they saw the difference between that heart and the hardened hearts of those who would not believe God. These disciples witnessed something they would never forget.

Another thing we witness in His response is that this woman had faith enough to go to Christ and make an appeal on behalf of her daughter. He fanned the flame of her faith, by the way He dealt with her, causing it to grow and enlarge until finally He said, *"O woman, great is thy faith."*

In the beginning, I do not think He would have said, *"O woman, great is thy faith."* When we bring our requests to the Lord and immediately do not get the answers we desire, we think, "Is God ever going to come through?" It may be that the Lord certainly is going to come through, but He is working on our faith, working in our lives, working in our hearts to increase our faith, to trust Him for even greater things than we ever imagined we could trust Him for. This is how the Lord worked in the life of this woman.

The disciples responded to the woman's request as she cried out, *"O Lord, thou Son of David; my daughter is grievously vexed with a devil. But he answered her not a word. And his disciples came and besought him, saying, Send her away; for she crieth after us."* They were not saying, "Lord, help this woman because we have a burden for her." They were saying, "Lord, do something with her because she is getting on our nerves. She is bothering us. She is annoying us. We are tired of her. Help her. Do something with her."

> *When God is silent, it is not because He does not hear.*

There are people who seek help for others, only because they are annoyed with them. They want someone else to deal with their problems. The disciples showed such evil intent here as they besought Christ to deal with this woman.

The Bible says, *"And his disciples came and besought him, saying, Send her away; for she crieth after us."* They said, "She is embarrassing us. We don't want to be identified with her." In my Bible, I have drawn a line connecting the word *"disciples"* in verse twenty-three and the word *"he"* in verse twenty-four. The answer was meant for the disciples rather than the Syrophenician woman. *"But he answered and said, I am not sent but unto the lost sheep of the house of Israel."* When He said that to His disciples, she was there in their midst and she heard it. *"Then came she and worshipped him, saying, Lord, help me."*

Did you ever pray and try to tell God everything He should know? Did you ever hear someone pray and go through all the motions of telling God everything He should know? As you listened to him praying, you wondered why he thought he had to inform God of things He already knows.

The poor woman said, *"Lord, help me."* She was near Christ and she saw something in His eyes. Before we consider the next statement, I want you to realize that His desire was to help her. He was saying, "I love you. I am going to help you. I know your need and I am going to help you." She saw that in His eyes.

Christ had withdrawn Himself from a certain group. He met this Syrophenician woman and knew that they would have referred to her as a dog. She knew it too. As a matter of fact, they did not want to be near such a woman.

She said, *"Lord, help me."* *"But he answered and said, It is not meet to take the children's bread, and to cast it to dogs."* The word *"dogs"* in this verse does not refer to the dogs of the street that have no master. This particular word was used for a dog that was a pet, one that was loved by a family.

I would like to have heard the tone of His voice when He said this. I would like to have seen the expression on His face as He spoke these words. In my own mind, I hear a certain tender tone filled with love, and I see in the eyes of Jesus Christ a testimony to the heart of this woman that He loved her. By looking at Him and hearing Him, she knew already that He was the Savior and that He loved her.

When Christ talked about the lost sheep of the house of Israel, He was talking about His personal ministry and how He came to present Himself as King of the Jews. This is what the Gospel according to Matthew is all about. She cried out to Him as a Jew would cry out, *"O Lord, thou Son of David."* He made no response on the basis of being the Savior of the Jews and the King of the Jews, but when she said, *"Lord, help me,"* He heard the cry of a lost world and He met her need.

He came first, as the Bible says, to the Jew. Paul wrote in Romans 1:16, *"For I am not ashamed of the gospel of Christ: for it is the power of God unto salvation to every one that believeth; to the Jew first, and also to the Greek."* He came also to the Greek, this Syrophenician, Canaanite woman.

The woman said in verse twenty-seven, *"Truth, Lord: yet the dogs eat of the crumbs which fall from their masters' table."* She used the same expression Christ used. Do you remember how heavy her heart was for her daughter? Do you remember how great a burden she had for her daughter? The burden was still there, but she was conversing with the Son of God, talking about her need, listening to Him. She found that He was approachable.

The language Christ used, on the surface, would sound, to someone with no desire to understand, as if He were being cruel to her. He was not cruel, but He was bringing out the faith in this woman, enlarging it, fanning the flame of it until it grew; then He said, *"Great is thy faith."*

You should leave the geography in God's hands and trust Him for fruit wherever He leads you.

This is the way faith works in our lives. We go to God with a problem because of someone we love. Many times, the only thing we are interested in is God taking care of our need. "If the Lord would just touch my daughter, touch my son, touch my marriage, touch my home, provide for me the job I want." Having our needs met is all we are concerned about. It is not what He means to us. It is like running to a religious bank and making a withdrawal. It is all academic. "God, do something for me. You can do it. Do this. That is all I want." The Lord, in His response, works with us so that not only does He meet our needs, but we learn to love and trust Him more. Has He worked this way in your life? This is the way He worked in this woman's life.

The Bible says, *"And she said, Truth, Lord: yet the dogs eat of the crumbs which fall from their masters' table."* Notice where the apostrophe is on the word *"masters'."* She used the word in the plural–not one master, but many masters. She recognized that there had been many masters. She recognized her place as a Gentile. She recognized the Jews for whom God had come. She acknowledged that while the children, represented here by the Jews, got the food, the little pet dog that was beneath the table got the crumbs that fell from the children.

She said, "I know that I am not a Jew, and that You are the Son of David, the Savior of the Jews. I see this, but I am willing to acknowledge that I am like one of those little dogs You talked about. I am standing here anxiously waiting to get any crumb that falls off the table." She said, "If You just give me a crumb, that is all I want." She believed now with greater faith than she ever had.

Let us look at the disciples again. They were shocked. They expected to find that kind of faith among the Jews, but they did not expect to find it among the Syrophenicians. The Lord did something in their hearts that they would long remember even after He had ascended to glory where *"he ever liveth to make intercession for them."*

When they thought about some place that does not hold the promise of much fruit, God proved to His followers, "Leave it in My hands and I will prove to you that I can go to a place among these Gentiles, a place where you expect nothing, and find a precious treasure you never thought existed–someone who would put great faith in Me."

Some of you may be thinking about some well-known place where you want to serve God. The truth is, you should leave the geography in God's hands and trust Him for fruit wherever He leads you.

THE REWARD FOR HER FAITH

The Bible says in verse twenty-eight, *"Then Jesus answered and said unto her, O woman, great is thy faith: be it unto thee even as thou wilt. And her daughter was made whole from that very hour."* Not only did her daughter have the devil cast out, but her faith was also rewarded. Most commentaries would call this the first of the Gentile converts.

There is no small work for God, and there are no little people. There is nothing insignificant. The Lord gives us this miraculous story of the Syrophenician to remind us of what great things our Savior can do.

In Matthew 15:29 the Bible says, *"And Jesus departed from thence, and came nigh unto the sea of Galilee; and went up into a mountain, and sat down there. And great multitudes came unto him."* If you were to study the commentaries, this multitude would not be described as the same kind of group the Lord Jesus found in Judea; it was not the same kind of group that was made up of converted Jews who followed Him. This was a group that was an outgrowth of the great faith in this Syrophenician woman. Do you see what the Son of God was doing? He was not only meeting the needs of people, but He was also proving to His followers how His work was to be done.

Many times those of us in the ministry will size up a person. We see a person with an earned degree or a graduate degree or a person of great means, and we think, "If I could just get that person to follow the Lord Jesus."

Do you see what happens to us? We start looking at things the way men look at things instead of the way God looks at things. It is not the greatness of people or even the potential of people we are to talk so much about; it is the greatness of God and the fact that all things are possible with God. There is no small work for God, and there are no little people. There is nothing insignificant. The Lord gives us this miraculous story of the Syrophenician to remind us of what great things our Savior can do.

Many years ago, I was pastoring a church in Lenoir City, Tennessee, and a weak, anemic-looking couple came through the door to attend one of the services. When I first saw them, I wondered what kind of handout they wanted. I figured we would be spending much time in our ministry helping them with some sort of religious-type welfare.

I was in for a great surprise. These people were having a difficult time in life and were dealing with severe physical problems. They came to our church with a great burden and a great heart. They were capable of loving and feeling and expressing emotion with depth that very few people have. The Lord did a soul-winning work through those people. They started a work in that church, and there have been more people come to Christ through the years as a result of their ministry than any other single thing in the life of that church.

I would have passed over them. The truth is, I would have been like those disciples wondering what could be done to get them off our backs. I am glad that the Lord does not look at people that way. Thank God this is not the way He looks at us.

Chapter Four

HAVE COMPASSION ON US

 here is a world of people in need. They are in a time of desperate need. As we read in the ninth chapter of the Gospel according to Mark, we find the Lord Jesus returning from the Mount of Transfiguration where He had been with three of His disciples, Peter, James, and John. He came into a valley upon a scene that represented great need.

The Bible says in Mark 9:14-29,

> *And when he came to his disciples, he saw a great multitude about them, and the scribes questioning with them. And straightway all the people, when they beheld him, were greatly amazed, and running to him saluted him. And he asked the scribes, What question ye with them? And one of the multitude answered and said, Master, I have brought unto thee my son, which hath a dumb spirit; and wheresoever he taketh*

him, he teareth him: and he foameth, and gnasheth with his teeth, and pineth away: and I spake to thy disciples that they should cast him out; and they could not. He answereth him, and saith, O faithless generation, how long shall I be with you? how long shall I suffer you? bring him unto me. And they brought him unto him: and when he saw him, straightway the spirit tare him; and he fell on the ground, and wallowed foaming. And he asked his father, How long is it ago since this came unto him? And he said, Of a child. And ofttimes it hath cast him into the fire, and into the waters, to destroy him: but if thou canst do any thing, have compassion on us, and help us. Jesus said unto him, If thou canst believe, all things are possible to him that believeth. And straightway the father of the child cried out, and said with tears, Lord, I believe; help thou mine unbelief. When Jesus saw that the people came running together, he rebuked the foul spirit, saying unto him, Thou dumb and deaf spirit, I charge thee, come out of him, and enter no more into him. And the spirit cried, and rent him sore, and came out of him: and he was as one dead; insomuch that many said, He is dead. But Jesus took him by the hand, and lifted him up; and he arose. And when he was come into the house, his disciples asked him privately, Why could not we cast him out? And he said unto them, This kind can come forth by nothing, but by prayer and fasting.

Notice the expression found in verse twenty-two, *"Have compassion on us."* Compassion means to have the hurt of others in our hearts. The man was saying to Christ, "Hurt with us. Care for us." If he only knew how much the Lord Jesus really did care. We will never plunge the depth, the height, or the breadth of His love.

Christ's love cannot be measured with some sort of measuring rod. He cares for us and loves us with an everlasting love.

In great agony the man said, *"Have compassion on us."* It was the boy who was suffering so, but if you have children, you understand that no child hurts without his parents hurting. The Lord heard that pitiful plea.

Remember that Christ had been on the Mount of Transfiguration. Before going to this mountain, He began to teach His disciples how He was going to bleed and die. The Bible says in Mark 8:31, *"And he began to teach them, that the Son of man must suffer many things, and be rejected of the elders, and of the chief priests, and scribes, and be killed, and after three days rise again."* He was not going to rule and reign at that time.

> *As our world becomes more faithless, as our generation becomes more faithless, what greater opportunity Satan has.*

We find their response in verse thirty-two. The Bible says in Mark 8:32-33, *"And he spake that saying openly. And Peter took him, and began to rebuke him. But when he had turned about and looked on his disciples, he rebuked Peter, saying, Get thee behind me, Satan: for thou savourest not the things that be of God, but the things that be of men."*

What Peter said was not of God; he was speaking the things of man. There is a world of difference between the things of God and things of man. When the disciples heard Christ speak, they could not believe what He said. That was a number of days before this particular miracle in Mark chapter nine, but their unbelief held a grip on them.

We can read in the Word of God that prior to this time, the disciples had been able to cast out demons. However, on this occasion, they failed. Notice what our Lord said when confronted with these people. In Mark 9:19 He said, *"O faithless generation."*

The highest thing we can do as human beings is to put our faith in the true and living God. There is nothing greater. God made us to faith Him, to trust Him, to believe Him. With faith, what marvelous things we can witness.

The Lord Jesus said, *"O faithless generation."* He found no faith in the scribes who were the religious leaders of their day. There was no real faith in the man who came with his son. The son had physical ailments and, in addition to that, was demon possessed. There was no faith in the boy.

The Lord Jesus also found no faith in His own disciples. What a tragedy! At times, we look outside our church family and declare how terrible it is living in a faithless generation and seeing people all about us who do not trust God. But God looks at those of us who are following Him, and He must say of us many times, "You are also faithless, not trusting Me, not believing Me. O faithless generation."

Think for a moment how the Holy Spirit can be operative in a faith environment, how we give the Lord liberty and do not limit Him as we trust Him and believe Him. But on the other side of that, think how we give the Devil opportunity in a faithless situation.

As our world becomes more faithless, as our generation becomes more faithless, what greater opportunity Satan has. As evil men and seducers wax worse and worse, we need to remember this. The Devil has great opportunity to work because of the increasing faithlessness of our generation.

Christ came down from the mountain where He was transfigured, and He saw the scribes questioning with His disciples and this pitiful man and his son. He cried out, *"O faithless generation, how long shall I be with you? how long shall I suffer you? bring him unto me."*

May God stir our hearts to believe Him, to trust Him. My desire is to see God do a mighty work in this generation. It is not going to be done without faith, believing and trusting Christ.

THE DISTURBING SCRIBES

These scribes were like beasts who had found a weak prey. The Word of God says in verse fourteen, *"And when he came to his disciples, he saw a great multitude about them, and the scribes questioning with them."* As you read the story, you understand that the man had already brought his boy to the disciples hoping to find Christ. Instead, he found the nine disciples that Christ left at the foot of the mountain. When he brought his pitiful child to the disciples for help, they could not do anything for him.

The scribes and the religious leaders saw this as their opportunity to mock, to ridicule, and to offer their sarcasm and opinions. This was a pitiful sight to behold–this man, brokenhearted; this child, in such terrible condition; and these disturbing scribes who cared nothing for the man or his son. They took keen delight in mocking the followers of the Lord Jesus as they witnessed their human weakness and displayed their inability to help the father and his son.

When the Lord Jesus came upon the scene, He put them to silence in this manner. Mark 9:16 says, *"And he asked the scribes, What question ye with them?"* Where there had been scoffing and ridiculing, there came a death-like hush. He saw His disciples surrounded by these scribes, and He spoke with a voice of authority, *"What question ye with them?"* Immediately, there was silence.

How many times have we gotten ourselves into a situation of faithless living? How often have we brought reproach upon our Christian testimony and upon our Lord because of our unbelief? How many times have we gotten into a situation where we would not trust the Lord and it seemed that all hope was gone? The world and its crowd of unbelievers scoffed at us until the Lord Jesus made a visit and put everyone to silence. What we need is a heavenly visitation. What we need is the Lord to come upon the scene. We need for God to work.

THE DESPERATE FATHER

The Bible says in Mark 9:19-21,

> *O faithless generation, how long shall I be with you? how long shall I suffer you? bring him unto me. And they brought him unto him: and when he saw him, straightway the spirit tare him; and he fell on the ground, and wallowed foaming. And he asked his father, How long is it ago since this came unto him? And he said, Of a child.*

Let us consider the record of this given in the Gospel according to Luke. The Bible says in Luke 9:37-38, *"And it came to pass, that on the next day, when they were come down from the hill, much people met him. And, behold, a man of the company cried out, saying, Master, I beseech thee, look upon my son: for he is mine only child."*

We have a record of this in the Gospel according to Matthew, Mark, and Luke. But here in Luke's record in verse thirty-eight of chapter nine, the Bible does not say he was just the man's child; the Bible says he was the *"only"* child the man had.

This father was desperate. He was hurting. Before we lose sight of this great truth, let us remember how many times in our lives that God has brought us to the point of desperation before we ever came to Him and trusted Him. How careless we become with our Christian life until God allows a burden so great we cannot do anything with it but bring it to Him.

Do you want to know what causes people to take the Lord at His word? He said in Matthew 11:28, *"Come unto me, all ye that labour and are heavy laden, and I will give you rest."* Do you know why we come to Him? We come because we cannot carry the load any longer. As long as we can carry it, we will carry it. When we fall beneath the crushing weight of it all, we cry out in desperation because we know the help that we need can only come from God.

THE DEMON-POSSESSED BOY

God's Word goes to a great deal of effort in describing this boy. Think about one of your children as you consider what the Bible says in Mark 9:17-18, *"And one of the multitude answered and said, Master, I have brought unto thee my son, which hath a dumb spirit."* The man began to describe what went on in the boy's life. He said, *"And wheresoever he taketh him, he teareth him:..."* In other words, the boy was not under his own control. He was demon possessed. *"...And he foameth, and gnasheth with his teeth,..."* Think of what this boy was going through and how his father was suffering as people ridiculed his child. The Bible says, *"...and pineth away."* The boy was dying.

Mark 9:20 says, *"And they brought him unto him: and when he saw him, straightway the spirit tare him; and he fell on the ground, and wallowed foaming."* He was like an animal. This was a human being, but he was like an animal. He was gnashing at his teeth. The demon spirit was tearing at him inside. There seemed to be a volcanic eruption inside the body of this human being, and he was foaming at the mouth like a mad dog.

How careless we become with our Christian life until God allows a burden so great we cannot do anything with it but bring it to Him.

Then the pitiful father said in verse twenty-two, *"And ofttimes it hath cast him into the fire."* He said, *"ofttimes."* Not just every once in a while, but many times it had cast him into the fire. No doubt, the boy's body was scarred from burns.

How many times did the father have to cast his own body on the child to put out the fire, to keep the child alive? He must have had to watch him night and day since he did not know what might happen to him. His body must have looked abused and scarred. Every time the father saw one of those scars and thought of the fires that the boy had gone into, his heart must have hurt.

The father said it had cast him *"into the waters."* The boy, of course, would not exercise the muscular control to swim, the coordination to spare his life when he got into the water. The father said it had cast him into the water. By that he meant, "I had to go in after him, to rescue him, to save his life, to pull him from the waters before he drowned."

Satan's objective was to destroy him. The father thought about this tearing, wallowing, foaming, fires, scars, and near drowning. No wonder the poor man said, *"If thou canst do any thing, have compassion on us, and help us."*

Imagine the hard hearts of those religious leaders who did not care for the man and his son. They took such keen delight in ridiculing the disciples; they did not care at all about the boy. I cannot imagine anyone not hurting for that child. But we can get so preoccupied with our problems and our petty concerns that we forget the great hurt and heartache of a dying world–a world without Christ, headed to hell.

One million, four hundred thousand people die every day, the majority of whom have never heard the name of Jesus. Yet we have Bibles on shelves that we never open. Before we condemn those scribes too severely, we need to think about the hardness of our own hearts toward the need of a lost and dying world.

Not only to Christ, but to all of us, the world cries, "Have compassion on us. Let our hurt get in your heart." We must give our lives away by yielding them to God. If we save our lives for ourselves, we will lose them. If we give our lives to Christ, He will bless and use us.

The Bible says in verses twenty-three and twenty-four, *"Jesus said unto him, If thou canst believe, all things are possible to him that believeth. And straightway the father of the child cried out, and said with tears, Lord, I believe;..."* In that moment he trusted the Lord. But he said, *"...help thou mine unbelief."*

> *We can get so preoccupied with our problems and our petty concerns that we forget the great hurt and heartache of a dying world–a world without Christ, headed to hell.*

In other words he said, "Oh God, I want this so badly. I want this to happen so badly. My son is so desperate. I am so desperate. I need help, but I have nowhere else to turn. We have become the attraction of this side show with these screaming, hard-hearted, careless scribes and these failing disciples. We need help, but I am haunted with so much unbelief. The years have taken their toll. I have hoped so long in vain. I have sought help so many times. My heart has sunk again. They tried and could not help my boy. Oh God, I am churning inside. I believe You, but I have such unbelief." This father said, *"Help thou mine unbelief."*

What is the Lord looking for in our lives? He is looking for faith. You may say, "I don't have much faith." Look to Christ and believe Him.

The Bible says in Mark 9:25-26,

> *When Jesus saw that the people came running together, he rebuked the foul spirit, saying unto him, Thou dumb and deaf spirit, I charge thee, come out of him, and enter no more into him. And the spirit cried, and rent him sore, and came out of him: and he was as one dead; insomuch that many said, He is dead.*

This demon was like a tenant leaving a rented apartment or a place where he has been living. He will not pay his rent, and to get even with the people who tell him it is time for him to go, he knocks holes in the walls, kicks the doors down, and rips the light fixtures out. The Lord Jesus commanded the demon, *"Come out of him, and enter no more into him."* But on his way out, he tried to destroy the boy and kill him. The people thought the boy was dead.

One million, four hundred thousand people die every day, the majority of whom have never heard the name of Jesus. Yet we have Bibles on shelves that we never open.

Verse twenty-seven is precious, *"But Jesus took him by the hand, and lifted him up; and he arose."* There are some people who think they are about dead, finished. There is nothing left. The Devil is finished with them. I wonder how many young people across America, how many young people on our major university campuses, have tried it all, done it all, and have exhausted themselves in sinful behavior. There is nothing left but a pile of flesh. I want to say to them, "The Lord Jesus still loves you; He is seeking you and desires to be your Savior."

The Bible says in verses twenty-eight and twenty-nine, *"And when he was come into the house, his disciples asked him privately, Why could not we cast him out? And he said unto them, This kind can come forth by nothing, but by prayer and fasting."* It costs something.

Do you remember, earlier on, the disciples heard Christ say He was going to bleed and die, and they rebuked Him? They let that thought wear on them until it affected their faith. It affected their belief. They could not do what they were called upon to do.

This is what happens to you and me. We let things wear on us and weaken us as Christians. As followers of the Lord, we let things trouble us. We may have never gotten over an incident that happened five years ago, three years ago, three months ago, or three weeks ago. The only problem is, we are not the Christians we once were. It is time to take care of those things.

Christ said, *"But by prayer and fasting."* Have you ever gotten to the place with something in your life where you knew you had no place to go but to Christ? The only One you could look to was the Lord? If you have ever been there and you have ever done that, you know He has never failed you. Oh, how much He cares. Look to God alone!

This father cried, *"Have compassion on us."* He does. Without question, He does. Trust the Lord Jesus like that father trusted Him. Trust Him now!

MONEY IN THE
MOUTH OF THE FISH

ur Lord works in very deliberate ways to prepare individuals to serve Him. What is happening in your life to prove that God is able? As we look at this miracle, we see in context that the Lord had been working in the life of Peter. In Matthew chapter sixteen, we read of Peter's great confession. The Bible says in Matthew 16:13-18,

> *When Jesus came into the coasts of Cæsarea Philippi, he asked his disciples, saying, Whom do men say that I the Son of man am? And they said, Some say that thou art John the Baptist: some, Elias; and others, Jeremias, or one of the prophets. He saith unto them, But whom say ye that I am? And Simon Peter answered and said, Thou art the Christ, the Son of the living God. And Jesus answered and said unto him, Blessed art thou, Simon Bar-jona: for flesh and blood hath not*

revealed it unto thee, but my Father which is in heaven. And I say also unto thee, That thou art Peter, and upon this rock I will build my church; and the gates of hell shall not prevail against it.

In the seventeenth chapter of the Gospel according to Matthew, we read about the marvelous Transfiguration of Jesus Christ. He went up into that high mountain and was transfigured in the presence of three of His disciples, Peter, James, and John. Moses and Elijah came to stand alongside the transfigured Christ. Peter was in the midst of all this. He was on a spiritual high. They came down from the mountain and traveled to Capernaum. This leads us to the miracle found in Matthew 17:24-27. God's Word says,

> *And when they were come to Capernaum, they that received tribute money came to Peter, and said, Doth not your master pay tribute? He saith, Yes. And when he was come into the house, Jesus prevented him, saying, What thinkest thou, Simon? of whom do the kings of the earth take custom or tribute? of their own children, or of strangers? Peter saith unto him, Of strangers. Jesus saith unto him, Then are the children free. Notwithstanding, lest we should offend them, go thou to the sea, and cast an hook, and take up the fish that first cometh up; and when thou hast opened his mouth, thou shalt find a piece of money: that take, and give unto them for me and thee.*

Peter was going fishing, but not for fish. In the hundreds of thousands of fish that were swimming in the Sea of Galilee, Peter threw in a hook, and one took the hook. He pulled it up, reached into its mouth, and found the money that they needed.

PAYMENT DUE

Notice the expression the Bible gives us in verse twenty-seven, *"When thou hast opened his mouth, thou shalt find a piece of money."* There was a payment due, and the money to make the payment was to be found in the mouth of the fish.

The Bible says in verse twenty-four, *"And when they were come to Capernaum, they that received tribute money came to Peter, and said, Doth not your master pay tribute?"* There is nothing here by coincidence. Everything is by purpose. These were not publicans collecting for the government; this particular tribute had nothing to do with Caesar. This was money that was collected by the Jews for the support of the temple, for the work of the Lord.

It was no accident that they came to Peter. In working with His disciples, the Lord Jesus chose one man to be the leader of the whole group. In Luke 22:31 the Lord said to Peter, *"Simon, Simon, behold, Satan hath desired to have you, that he may sift you as wheat."* The word *"sift"* means "to move up and down."

Christ told Peter, "You're going to deny Me; you will deny Me three times before the cock crows." The Lord Jesus told Peter of a low hour in life, but in the same breath He said, *"But...when thou art converted, strengthen thy brethren."*

It was Peter who answered the Lord in Matthew sixteen, and the Lord answered back in verse eighteen, *"Upon this rock I will build my church; and the gates of hell shall not prevail against it."* Peter was one of those disciples chosen to go and see the miracle performed on the daughter of Jairus while the others stood outside. Peter, James, and John were the three that went up into the high mountain when the Lord Jesus was transfigured. Peter saw Christ in the glorious likeness that He shall come in, clothed in the glory of God. Peter heard God say, *"This is my beloved Son,... hear ye him."*

The religious leaders came to Peter. Remember, Peter had a fishing business on the north of the Galilee and was well known in the area of Capernaum. These religious leaders who gathered tribute for the temple approached Peter and said, "Does not your master pay the temple tribute?" They reminded Peter that payment was due.

Let us get the Old Testament background for this particular part of the story. In the book of Exodus, the thirtieth chapter, God established the principle of giving to His work. In Exodus 30:11-16 the Bible says, *"And the LORD spake unto Moses, saying, When thou takest the sum of the children of Israel after their number, then shall they give every man a ransom for his soul unto the LORD..."* Notice the expression, *"every man a ransom for his soul unto the LORD."* This money represented something. It was a picture of something. The Bible says,

> *...when thou numberest them; that there be no plague among them, when thou numberest them. This they shall give, every one that passeth among them that are numbered, half a shekel after the shekel of the sanctuary: (a shekel is twenty gerahs:) an half shekel shall be the offering of the LORD. Every one that passeth among them that are numbered, from twenty years old and above, shall give an offering unto the LORD.*

The Bible says, *"twenty years old and above."* God considered that the people were fully accountable for this tribute money at age twenty.

"The rich shall not give more, and the poor shall not give less than half a shekel, when they give an offering unto the LORD, to make an atonement for your souls." Note the expression, *"atonement for your souls."* God's Word continues,

> *And thou shalt take the atonement money of the children of Israel, and shalt appoint it for the service*

> *of the tabernacle of the congregation; that it may be*
> *a memorial unto the children of Israel before the*
> *LORD, to make an atonement for your souls.*

Every adult Jew was to give tribute money for the support of the work of the Lord; in particular, for the work of the tabernacle and for keeping the tabernacle as it should be. It was a substitute offering in this sense; it was given instead of going and doing work there. It was a representative offering. The *"atonement for your souls"* refers to the work of God done in the work of the tabernacle.

Let us look again in the book of Nehemiah, chapter ten. Remember that in the book of Exodus they had the tabernacle, and the offering was given for the work of the tabernacle. In the book of Nehemiah, they had gone from the tabernacle to the temple. Those returning from the exile were to give an offering for the work to be done in the temple. The Bible says in Nehemiah 10:32-33,

> *Also we made ordinances for us, to charge*
> *ourselves yearly with the third part of a shekel for the*
> *service of the house of our God; for the shewbread,*
> *and for the continual meat offering, and for the*
> *continual burnt offering, of the sabbaths, of the new*
> *moons, for the set feasts, and for the holy things, and*
> *for the sin offerings to make an atonement for Israel,*
> *and for all the work of the house of our God.*

There was a payment due from all of the Jews, twenty years old and older. This was not a civil payment; it had nothing to do with the government. In the time of our Lord, it had nothing to do with Rome. This was a religious tribute given to the work of God, an offering given to God for God's temple.

Before coming back to our story, let us look at the book of Malachi chapter three. The Bible says in verse one, *"Behold, I will send my messenger, and he shall prepare the way before me: and the Lord, whom ye seek, shall suddenly come to his temple..."* In Malachi chapter three and verse one, note the expression *"his temple."* Whose temple was it? It was His temple. If we are going to understand the lesson of this miracle, we need to understand whose temple this was for which they were taking money. It was the Lord's temple, *"...even the messenger of the covenant, whom ye delight in: behold, he shall come, saith the LORD of hosts."*

In Matthew chapter seventeen, we find that payment was due. These religious leaders, who had nothing to do with the Caesar, came and asked if the Lord Jesus, as a male adult, an Israelite, was going to support the work of God in the temple of God. An offering had been established to be given every year for the work of the Lord. Payment was due.

PAYMENT PROMISED

The Bible says in Matthew 17:25, *"He saith, Yes..."* Peter answered for the Lord, *"Yes."* Payment was promised. Evidently, Peter began to think about what he had promised. He thought to himself, "I should have asked the Lord Jesus about this."

Did you ever speak that way? Peter remembered that Christ was in a house and now he had to go to the house to explain to Him what he had gotten the whole crowd into because he had already said, "Yes, the Lord is going to do this." God was going to give money to God. This is not normally the way it works.

Peter had just declared in Caesarea Philippi that the Lord Jesus was the Son of God, and the temple was the Lord's. Now as he had spoken he knew that he had gotten ahead of the whole thing by saying, "Yes, God is going to give money to God." The Bible says, *"He saith, Yes. And when he was come into the house, Jesus prevented him."* What does that mean? What do you think Peter wanted to do? He wanted to talk. Before he could say a word, the Lord Jesus talked to him.

All of us have a problem of talking more than we should be talking and getting ahead of God with our talking. This amounts to presuming on the Lord. Peter was going to be reminded of something: that the Lord Jesus knows everything.

Christ prevented Peter, and then He said, *"What thinkest thou, Simon? of whom do the kings of the earth take custom or tribute? of their own children, or of strangers?"* If one reads this properly, the emphasis is on *"earth."* We should make note that this particular miracle is recorded only in the Gospel according to Matthew, which is the Gospel of the kingdom. The Lord Jesus made a comparison between the King of heaven and earth and the kings of the earth.

Whose temple was it? It was His temple. If we are going to understand the lesson of this miracle, we need to understand whose temple this was for which they were taking money.

Christ asked Peter, *"What thinkest thou, Simon? of whom do the kings of the earth take custom or tribute? of their own children, or of strangers? Peter saith unto him, Of strangers. Jesus saith unto him, Then are the children free."* What does all of this mean? Christ explained that if you find someone with a palace, an empire, or a kingdom, do they take tribute support from their own family, or do they take tribute and support from strangers? In other words, does a king of the earth ask the prince and princesses to support his palace and his work, or does he take tribute from strangers? This is an easy question to answer. The royal family does not take tribute from their own; they do not ask it of their own children. They take tribute from strangers.

Christ was reminding Peter of something. He was reminding Peter that the temple was the Lord's and that Jesus Christ is God. He said to Peter, "Do you understand now, Peter, that the Son of God does not give to the work of God? The Son of God is coequal, coexistent, eternally existent with God the Father. Do you understand that?" Peter got the message.

God was going to give money to God. This is not normally the way it works.

Then the Lord said, *"Nothwithstanding, lest we should offend them, go thou to the sea, and cast a hook, and take up the fish that first cometh up; and when thou hast opened his mouth, thou shalt find a piece of money: that take, and give unto them for me and thee."* Christ said, *"Notwithstanding, lest we should offend them."* The Lord Jesus willingly submitted to this law, though He did not have to submit to it. He was willing to humble Himself in obedience to this law, though He did not have to do it because He is God.

PAYMENT MADE

Christ said, *"Go thou."* I have Peter circled in verse twenty-four in my Bible, and I have those two words *"go thou"* circled in verse twenty-seven. I have a line connecting the two because I want to understand how important it is for people who desire the Lord to use them in a special way to realize that God deals with them in a special way.

Some of you are going through something at this moment, and you wonder why you are going through it. God wants to use you in a way that is out of the ordinary. He allows something in your life that He does not allow in just anyone's life because He intends to do something with your life that He is not going to do with everyone else. Peter was allowed to see things that others did not see. Peter was allowed to do things that others did not do because Christ literally chose Peter to be the next pastor of the disciples. He worked intimately with Peter preparing him, strengthening his faith, and making him into the man that He desired for him to be.

Christ said, "Now Peter, they came to you. You said this. You understand that I am God and God does not have to give tribute to God. But I want you, so that they will not be offended, to go and cast a hook into the sea. There is going to be one fish out of the hundreds of thousands that will take that hook. When it does, pull it up, reach into its mouth, and take the coin that is the exact amount needed to pay this tribute."

Christ is the God of everything in heaven and earth. He knew every part of the conversation Peter had with the religious leaders. He knew every word that Peter had spoken. He knew the promise that Peter had made. He knew exactly what Peter needed to hear and learn because of the promise he made to those religious leaders, the tribute collectors. He knew that Peter could be strengthened by going down to the seaside in Capernaum, casting a hook into the sea, and pulling up the fish that took the hook, reaching inside, and finding the exact coin that was needed to pay the tribute.

> *The Lord Jesus made a comparison between the King of heaven and earth and the kings of the earth.*

Can you imagine Peter leaving the presence of Jesus Christ, going down there, taking a hook, and casting the hook into the sea? Suddenly a fish bit the hook, and as Peter pulled the fish to shore, he took the fish in hand, reached inside its mouth, and found a coin. When he pulled it out to the light of day, he saw that it was exactly the coin needed. Undoubtedly, Peter was praising God and saying, "God not only knows everything, He can do all things. Jesus Christ is God."

What does that coin mean? Why was that offering established? What did that substitute offering represent? Why was it being received?

Notice the language of the Lord Jesus, *"Thou shalt find a piece of money: that take, and give unto them for me and thee."* Christ needed no ransom. He did not need to be redeemed. The little word *"for"* means "in the place of; as a substitute; to provide for."

Christ said, *"Give unto them for me and thee."* Our Lord identified Himself with Peter here, but not just with the coin being paid in tribute for the temple of God. He identified Himself with Peter as a sinner on the cross when He paid our ransom in His precious blood, redeeming us by His own blood. II Corinthians 5:21 says, *"For he hath made him to be sin for us, who knew no sin; that we might be made the righteousness of God in him."*

> *Christ was reminding Peter of something. He was reminding Peter that the temple is the Lord's and that Jesus Christ is God.*

Do you know what Christ was teaching Peter in this miracle with the money? He was not only teaching him that He knows all things and that He is in control of all things, but He was teaching him something about the redeeming blood of Christ and the ransom of his soul. Perhaps Peter was reminded of the fish incident when the Spirit of God gave him the words to pen in I Peter 1:18-19. The Bible says, *"Forasmuch as ye know that ye were not redeemed with corruptible things, as silver and gold, from your vain conversation received by tradition from your fathers; but with the precious blood of Christ, as of a lamb without blemish and without spot."*

Maybe as the Spirit of God led Peter to pen these words, *"not redeemed with corruptible things, as silver and gold,"* a little light went on in his mind and he remembered the day on the seashore when he held the silver and gold in his hand that represented atonement. But he was reminded here that it is not with silver and gold, it is with the precious blood of Jesus Christ that we are redeemed.

It is marvelous what God teaches us from a simple little fish story. There is payment due. God said, "The whole world has been found guilty." There is a promise made. God promised in His Word that He would send a Redeemer. There is payment made. The Lord Jesus said on the cross, *"It is finished."* That is what this miracle is all about.

Chapter Six

WHILE IT IS DAY

he greatest commentary on the Bible is the Bible. If you want to know what the Bible is teaching, and you have trouble understanding a passage, compare it with other passages. As you compare Scripture with Scripture, God will give you understanding of what a passage means.

As we continue to look at the miracles of Jesus, may the Lord help us to see beyond the miracle to the Bible lesson that the Lord has for us. The Bible says in John 9:1-7,

> *And as Jesus passed by, he saw a man which was blind from his birth. And his disciples asked him, saying, Master, who did sin, this man, or his parents, that he was born blind? Jesus answered, Neither hath this man sinned, nor his parents: but that the works of God should be made manifest in him. I must work the works of him that sent me, while it is day: the night cometh, when no man can work. As long as I am in the world, I am the light*

of the world. When he had thus spoken, he spat on the ground, and made clay of the spittle, and he anointed the eyes of the blind man with the clay, and said unto him, Go, wash in the pool of Siloam, (which is by interpretation, Sent.) He went his way therefore, and washed, and came seeing.

Notice the expression that our Lord gives us in the fourth verse of this ninth chapter when Christ said, *"While it is day."* When we consider this expression *"day,"* we are considering a time of opportunity. *"I must work the works of him that sent me, while it is day:..."* or while there is opportunity. *"...the night cometh, when no man can work."* Many people waste their opportunity. They fail to seize the moment or moments that God gives to get His work accomplished.

Let us consider what we find in John 6:28-29. The Bible says, *"Then said they unto him, What shall we do, that we might work the works of God? Jesus answered and said unto them, This is the work of God, that ye believe on him whom he hath sent."* Remember, Christ said in John 9:4, *"I must work the works of him that sent me, while it is day: the night cometh, when no man can work."*

The Lord spoke in John chapter nine of doing the works of Him that sent Him. *"I must work the works of him that sent me."* I do not want you to make the mistake of thinking that healing a blind man is the work of Him that sent Him. The Bible says very clearly in John 6:28-29, *"Then said they unto him, What shall we do, that we might work the works of God? Jesus answered and said unto them, This is the work of God, that ye believe on him whom he hath sent."*

THE LIGHT OF THE WORLD

There are many things going on in the life of every human being. We have a God who seizes every opportunity to do His work in that

person's life *"while it is day,"* while there is opportunity. No matter where the Lord may begin, no matter where the Lord may enter, no matter where the Lord may start working in a person, the work that He desires to do is just what the Bible says, it is the work of salvation. Let us keep this in mind as we move through this entire ninth chapter of the Gospel according to John.

Notice that the Lord Jesus said of Himself in John 9:5, *"I am the light of the world."* Some may say, "People need light." Yes, they need light, but they also need sight. He is the Light of the World, and He is present in the world in the Person of the Holy Spirit. He is moving and working, wooing and winning, calling out a bride. He is the light of the world, yet men still walk in darkness. They must have light, but they also must have sight.

As we begin to read this chapter, we discover that there are two types of blindness. *"And as Jesus passed by, he saw a man which was blind from his birth."* I want you to notice the word *"and"* telling us that this particular story is connected with what we find just previous. Notice also the expression *"he saw a man."* Because the man was blind, we know that he could not possibly have seen the Lord Jesus. Even if the man had physical sight, we should not assume that he would have seen Christ. The point that the Bible makes is not that the man saw Christ, but that Christ saw him. The Lord saw him.

There are many times in life when we are in a situation where it seems that we cannot see Christ, but there is never a moment in life when Christ does not see us. There are times in our Christian lives when things are so clouded that it seems as though we cannot see Him, but there has never been a moment in our lives, even before we were saved, that Christ did not see us.

As the Lord Jesus traveled with His disciples, the Bible says, *"He saw a man which was blind from his birth."* Notice how foolish His disciples were. This reminds me so much of my own foolishness. *"And his disciples asked him, saying, Master, who did sin, this man, or his parents, that he was born blind?"* Have you ever asked a question that really did not make any sense at all, and after a while, you realized how senseless a question it really was?

Consider their question again. When they saw the blind man, they were not moved with compassion as Christ was moved with compassion toward the man. They did not love him like the Lord Jesus loved him. They did not see him as Christ saw him. They did not see him in the same sense in which Christ saw him. They did not see through his physical blindness to his greatest need. They only became curious and wanted to talk about some philosophy, to question the reason for his blindness. They wanted to discuss the man's problem instead of doing something about it.

> *No matter where the Lord may begin, no matter where the Lord may enter, no matter where the Lord may start working in a person, the work that He desires to do is just what the Bible says, it is the work of salvation.*

We find so much of this today. Many people say, "I would like to give you my opinion. Would you like to give me your opinion?" Does anyone care about what people really need, or are we just interested in someone hearing our opinions? So often, we care more about what we say and who hears it than we do about helping anyone to know God.

The Lord answered, *"Neither hath this man sinned, nor his parents."* In other words, the reason for his blindness was not his sin or his parents' sin. He was not saying that the man and his parents were not sinners. He was saying that this blindness was not due to sin.

We should be cautious when we try to explain why "bad things" happen to people. In life, some things we choose are not right and some things we choose are right, but we make deliberate choices

with our lives. There are choices that God makes for us. We have no control over things that God allows to come into our lives.

On occasion I meet people who have some sort of physical infirmity or deformity. They did not choose that infirmity or deformity for themselves. If they are ever going to have any peace in life, they have to come to the realization that somehow and some way, God allowed it. Someone may blame a parent who passed a disease down to a child. When we try to come up with a specific answer to everyone's heartache and difficulty, we are running a risk–not just the risk of playing God, but the risk of having God deal with us to show us we are not God.

> *The point that the Bible makes is not that the man saw Christ, but that Christ saw him.*

The Lord Jesus said, "It wasn't his sin, and it wasn't his parents' sin. There is something greater here– *"that the works of God should be made manifest in him."* Do you believe that the works of God are marvelous? When the works of God are manifest, we should recognize that the works of God are marvelous. Keep this in mind as we move through this story.

The Lord said, "The reason this man is blind is that God is going to do a work in his life." Do you think it is possible that a man who was born blind could come to a place in his life when he would say, "Glory to God, I am so grateful I was blind. Because of my blindness, I've come to something I would never have come to had it not been for my blindness."

The Bible says in John 9:5-7,

> *As long as I am in the world, I am the light of the world. When he had thus spoken, he spat on the ground, and made clay of the spittle, and he anointed the eyes of the blind man with the clay, and said unto*

him, Go, wash in the pool of Siloam, (which is by interpretation, Sent.) He went his way therefore, and washed, and came seeing.

This is where the Lord Jesus started with this man. If you do not read this chapter through, you may think this is the end of the story. How wonderful that he could see; but remember, he could see physically, but there was a greater blindness. He was spiritually blind. In II Corinthians 4:3-4 the Bible says, *"But if our gospel be hid, it is hid to them that are lost: in whom the god of this world hath blinded the minds of them which believe not, lest the light of the glorious gospel of Christ, who is the image of God, should shine unto them."*

> *There are many times in life when we are in a situation where it seems that we cannot see Christ, but there is never a moment in life when Christ does not see us.*

Dealing with unsaved people, we wonder why they behave like they behave, why they speak like they speak, and why they go where they go. We must not forget that they are blind. Without Christ, a man is blind. When considering Christ and the work of God—which is much more than healing physical blindness—we would be disappointed if the story of this man stopped here. How many of us allow God to do only part of the work in our lives or only part of the work in the life of someone we love instead of doing the thorough work that He desires to do?

THE BLINDNESS OF THESE PHARISEES

Notice also in this passage the Pharisees and the way they responded to this man's physical sight. The Pharisees could never be happy and rejoice with him over the good thing that happened to him.

The Bible says as we continue in John 9:8, *"The neighbours therefore, and they which before had seen him that he was blind, said, Is not this he that sat and begged?"* This man was quite a famous beggar. They all knew him as a beggar. They said, "Isn't this the guy that sat and begged? Isn't this our neighbor that was a blind beggar?" The Bible continues in verses nine through nineteen,

> *Some said, This is he: others said, He is like him: but he said, I am he. Therefore said they unto him, How were thine eyes opened? He answered and said, A man that is called Jesus made clay, and anointed mine eyes, and said unto me, Go to the pool of Siloam, and wash: and I went and washed, and I received sight. Then said they unto him, Where is he? He said, I know not. They brought to the Pharisees him that aforetime was blind.*

Here was this blind beggar who, for the first time in his entire life, could see. They took him to the Pharisees. The Bible says it was the Sabbath day when the Lord Jesus made the clay and opened his eyes.

> *Then again the Pharisees also asked him how he had received his sight. He said unto them, He put clay upon mine eyes, and I washed, and do see. Therefore said some of the Pharisees, This man is not of God, because he keepeth not the sabbath day. Others said, How can a man that is a sinner do such miracles? And there was a division among them. They say unto the blind man again, What sayest thou of him, that he hath opened thine eyes? He said, He is a prophet. But the Jews did not believe concerning him, that he had been blind, and received his sight, until they called the parents of him that had received his sight. And they asked them, saying, Is this your son, who ye say was born blind? how then doth he now see?*

The Pharisees just did not understand. His parents knew they were in for trouble dealing with these Pharisees. The Bible says in verse twenty, *"His parents answered them and said, We know that this is our son, and that he was born blind: but by what means he now seeth, we know not; or who hath opened his eyes, we know not: he is of age; ask him: he shall speak for himself."*

I can appreciate the humorous side of the Holy Spirit in giving us this narrative as He does. Imagine the scene. The man received his sight and he ran into his neighbors. They were excited and they said, "Here is a guy who looks like our neighbor and talks like him, but this man can see. I can't understand this." Some of them said, "Well, I don't really think this is him." He said, "It's me! I have never seen you folks before, but I sure do recognize your voices and it's me. I am he." They said, "Well, we must get you to the Pharisees."

> *They wanted to discuss the man's problem instead of doing something about it.*

When the Pharisees saw him, they said, "You were healed on the Sabbath day." You would think that they would have said, "Praise God, you can see! I can't believe that after all these years! You were born blind and you have never been able to see a single thing. Let's rejoice! Here is a guy that can see!" They could not get happy about anything.

The Pharisees said, "We'd like to know who healed you on the Sabbath. Get your parents in here." The parents could tell by the attitude of these Pharisees that they were upset, so the parents said, "He's of age, ask him. He is old enough to answer for himself." The story continues in verses twenty-two through twenty-six,

> *These words spake his parents, because they feared the Jews: for the Jews had agreed already, that if any man did confess that he was Christ, he should be put*

*out of the synagogue. Therefore said his parents, He is
of age; ask him. Then again called they the man that
was blind, and said unto him, Give God the praise: we
know that this man is a sinner. He answered and said,
Whether he be a sinner or no, I know not: one thing I
know, that, whereas I was blind, now I see. Then said
they to him again, What did he to thee?*

Notice the language, *"What did he to thee?"* These Pharisees
could not even smile. They could not say one good thing about him
being able to see.

*"What did he to thee? how opened he thine eyes? He answered
them, I have told you already, and ye did not hear: wherefore would
ye hear it again?"* Then he ridiculed them. *"...will ye also be his
disciples?"* That infuriated the Pharisees.

John 9:28-30 says, *"Then they reviled him and said, Thou art his
disciple; but we are Moses' disciples. We know that God spake unto
Moses: as for this fellow, we know not from whence he is. The man
answered and said unto them, Why herein is a marvellous thing,..."*

Did we not say already that God's work is a marvelous thing? This
man finally got to the place where he said, "If you aren't going to
rejoice and praise God with me over me getting my eyesight, I'm
going to get excited about it myself. If you're not going to be thrilled
with it, I'm going to be thrilled with it. Let me tell you something, it
is a marvelous thing that has been done here."

The story continues in verses thirty through thirty-three,

*Why herein is a marvellous thing, that ye know not
from whence he is, and yet he hath opened mine eyes.
Now we know that God heareth not sinners: but if any
man be a worshipper of God, and doeth his will, him
he heareth. Since the world began was it not heard that*

*any man opened the eyes of one that was born blind. If
this man were not of God, he could do nothing.*

He said, "I want to tell you something. There is something special
that happened. Since the whole world began, nothing like this has
happened to anyone except to me, and I am going to rejoice over it
and praise God for it because I can see."

The Bible says in verse thirty-four, *"They answered and said unto
him, Thou wast altogether born in sins, and dost thou teach us? And
they cast him out."* They threw him out of the synagogue. There were
some castings out that were more serious than others. Some only
lasted for a thirty-day period, and some lasted longer. They told him
to get out and that he could not worship in the synagogue.

Is that not the way wicked men work? They could not understand.
In their darkness they refused to believe, so they just became
outraged and cast him out. Those of us who have lived a while have
seen people behave just like that. They were blind.

THE SIGHT OF THIS MAN

Let us see also in this passage the sight of this blind man. He had
not gotten his real sight yet. The Bible says that they cast him out.
Here was a sad situation. Everyone should have been rejoicing.
Everyone should have been thrilled, but they were not.

I can see the man now–dejected, cast out. Notice what the very
next verse says, *"Jesus heard that they had cast him out; and when
he had found him, he said unto him, Dost thou believe on the Son of
God?"* Others may cast you out, but the Lord Jesus will find you.
You may be rejected by an unbelieving crowd, but Jesus Christ sees
you and knows right where you are. You may think that you are so
far off the path you cannot find Him. Friend, you do not have to
worry about finding Him, He will find you.

I like to imagine this man. I like to imagine what kind of mental condition he was in when the Lord heard that the Pharisees had cast him out. Christ had told him when He put the spittle and clay on his eyes to go wash in the pool of Siloam. He could not have found his way to the pool of Siloam; he was still blind. The clay packed on his eyes hindered his sight even more. People had to guide him down to the pool. When they got him down there and washed his eyes, he could see. They took him back to his neighborhood, and his neighbors saw that he could see. They ran him over to the Pharisees, and he was ridiculed and cast out.

Have you ever been ill-received from someone you thought might receive you in a friendly way? Have you ever been disappointed the way something turned out? I want you to know that our disappointments are God's appointments. He will be there. The Bible says, *"And when he had found him, he said unto him, Dost thou believe on the Son of God? He answered and said, Who is he, Lord, that I might believe on him? And Jesus said unto him, Thou hast both seen him, and it is he that talketh with thee."* Can it be stated any more plainly than that?

Before we continue, we have to go back to see this fellow–begging, pitiful, blind from birth. The disciples needed to learn something. They needed to learn that there were more important things than discussing why a man was blind. They needed to learn more than just trying to discuss problems. We need to be people of action who allow God to work through us to accomplish His work in people's lives.

The work of God is not healing physical blindness. That is just the starting point. You may get sick and go to the hospital. You may know someone who has had a heart attack and gone to the hospital. You may know someone who is going through some tragic or disappointing thing in life and needs help. He needs family, love, and nurturing, and God uses that as an open door to start working on that person. But just helping him through his heartache or healing him in his sickness is not what God intends to do. He wants to do more than that. He wants to do the real work of God in his life. We need to press the matter. We need to discern when God has opened a door, and what He really intends to do. He wants people be saved.

This man said, *"Who is he, Lord, that I might believe on him? And Jesus said unto him, Thou hast both seen him, and it is he that talketh with thee. And he said, Lord, I believe. And he worshipped him."* This man got saved; this blind man received his sight. If the man lived today, he would say to us, "Don't feel sorry for me that I was born blind. If I had not been born blind, I would have never met the Lord Jesus. I would never have been saved and received my spiritual eyesight."

> *Our disappointments are God's appointments.*

There are many people out there suffering with some thing that they think is the worst thing. It is not the worst thing; the worst thing is if they die and go to hell. God could have allowed some thing that they call the worst thing, so He could do the best thing, which is to save their lost souls. May the Lord help us to see this through spiritual eyes.

Verse thirty-nine says, *"And Jesus said, For judgment I am come into this world, that they which see not might see; and that they which see might be made blind."* You have to realize that you are lost. You have to realize that you are blind before you can see. If you think you see without Christ, you are going to remain blind. If you do not realize that you are lost, and you think you can see, you are really blind. This is a great miracle. It is not a miracle of simply touching a blind man's physical blindness and making him see; it is a miracle that God used the man's blindness while it was day to save his lost soul.

THE PEOPLE REJOICED

I t is a wonderful thing to rejoice in the Lord. It is a terrible thing to get to the place where we cannot rejoice. There are many who even attend church regularly that have lost all sense of happiness in the Lord Jesus.

As people begin taking their eyes off the Lord and counting their troubles instead of their blessings, before long they are blinded to the goodness of God. They are puffed up with themselves and are no longer able to rejoice.

Let us look at this amazing miracle and see what the Lord Jesus did which caused the people to rejoice. In each miraculous account, God has a tremendous lesson for us.

Before Christ went to the cross to die for our sins, He spent the last months of His earthly ministry on the other side of the Jordan River. It was there that He came into a synagogue and made contact with a needy woman. The Bible gives us this story in Luke 13:10-17,

> *And he was teaching in one of the synagogues on the sabbath. And, behold, there was a woman which had a spirit of infirmity eighteen years, and was bowed together, and could in no wise lift up herself. And when Jesus saw her, he called her to him, and said unto her, Woman, thou art loosed from thine infirmity. And he laid his hands on her: and immediately she was made straight, and glorified God. And the ruler of the synagogue answered with indignation, because that Jesus had healed on the sabbath day, and said unto the people, There are six days in which men ought to work: in them therefore come and be healed, and not on the sabbath day. The Lord then answered him, and said, Thou hypocrite, doth not each one of you on the sabbath loose his ox or his ass from the stall, and lead him away to watering? And ought not this woman, being a daughter of Abraham, whom Satan hath bound, lo, these eighteen years, be loosed from this bond on the sabbath day? And when he had said these things, all his adversaries were ashamed: and all the people rejoiced for all the glorious things that were done by him.*

Notice the beautiful expression given to us in the seventeenth verse, *"the people rejoiced."* They rejoiced in what the Lord Jesus Christ had done.

THE CONDITION OF THE WOMAN

On the Sabbath day, the Lord Jesus entered the synagogue. We are not surprised by this because it was His custom. Look closely at the woman who came on the Sabbath day to worship God in that synagogue. The Bible says, *"And, behold, there was a woman which*

had a spirit of infirmity eighteen years, and was bowed together, and could in no wise lift up herself."

The Bible describes this woman as a woman who was bent over double. If you had come into that synagogue, she could not have greeted you. She could not have seen you. No doubt she did not even see the Lord Jesus, but He saw her.

She was in a certain section of the synagogue assigned to the women. Bowed over double, she had been looking at the ground for eighteen years. It is amazing to think of how she got into the place. The trip from where she lived to the synagogue would have been very difficult. Whatever the distance, it was a rough journey to take in the condition she was in. She came to the synagogue on the Sabbath to worship the Lord.

The Bible says in Luke 13:12-13, *"And when Jesus saw her, he called her to him, and said unto her, Woman, thou art loosed from thine infirmity. And he laid his hands on her: and immediately she was made straight, and glorified God."* In verse sixteen the Lord says, *"And ought not this woman, being a daughter of Abraham, whom Satan hath bound, lo, these eighteen years, be loosed from this bond on the sabbath day?"*

The word *"infirmity"* is used to describe this woman. When we get to the sixteenth verse, we find that as mysterious as it may sound, this condition came upon this woman because of the Devil. She was a woman of great faith in God. The Lord had allowed the Devil to lay this infirmity on this woman for eighteen years.

We are reminded of the story of Job. He was an upright man who feared God. The Bible says in Job 1:1, *"There was a man in the land of Uz, whose name was Job; and that man was perfect and upright, and one that feared God, and eschewed evil."*

Then the Devil appeared before the Lord in Job 1:6-12,

> *Now there was a day when the sons of God came to present themselves before the LORD, and Satan came also among them. And the LORD said unto Satan, Whence comest thou? Then Satan answered the LORD, and said, From going to and fro in the earth, and from walking up and down in it. And the LORD said unto Satan, Hast thou considered my servant Job, that there is none like him in the earth, a perfect and an upright man, one that feareth God, and escheweth evil? Then Satan answered the LORD, and said, Doth Job fear God for nought? Hast not thou made an hedge about him, and about his house, and about all that he hath on every side?...*

One does not put a fence around something he does not own. The Devil said to God, "You built a fence around him. You love him and he is Yours." The Devil was correct!

> *...thou hast blessed the work of his hands, and his substance is increased in the land. But put forth thine hand now, and touch all that he hath, and he will curse thee to thy face. And the LORD said unto Satan, Behold, all that he hath is in thy power; only upon himself put not forth thine hand. So Satan went forth from the presence of the LORD.*

Then the Bible says in Job 2:3-10,

> *And the LORD said unto Satan, Hast thou considered my servant Job, that there is none like him in the earth, a perfect and an upright man, one that feareth God, and escheweth evil? and still he holdeth fast his integrity, although thou movedst me against him, to*

*destroy him without cause. And Satan answered the
LORD, and said, Skin for skin, yea, all that a man hath
will he give for his life. But put forth thine hand now,
and touch his bone and his flesh, and he will curse thee
to thy face. And the LORD said unto Satan, Behold, he
is in thine hand; but save his life. So went Satan forth
from the presence of the LORD, and smote Job with sore
boils from the sole of his foot unto his crown. And he
took him a potsherd to scrape himself withal; and he
sat down among the ashes. Then said his wife unto
him, Dost thou still retain thine integrity? curse God,
and die. But he said unto her, Thou speakest as one of
the foolish women speaketh. What? shall we receive
good at the hand of God, and shall we not receive evil?
In all this did not Job sin with his lips.*

God allowed Satan to touch Job's body. The Bible is very clear in
Luke chapter thirteen. The Lord Jesus said, "This woman is in this
condition because Satan has bound her." In other words, the Lord
turned the Devil loose on this woman.

There is a special warning for us here. We should be careful about
trying to play God and making a decision with finality about why people
are suffering. We do not always know; we do not understand all these
things. But the Lord Jesus said, "The Devil has bound this woman."

THE CRITICISM OF THE RULER

The Bible says in Luke 13:14, *"And the ruler of the synagogue
answered with indignation, because that Jesus had healed on the
sabbath day, and said unto the people, There are six days in which
men ought to work: in them therefore come and be healed, and not on
the sabbath day."* Mark the little word *"ought,"* because the Lord
Jesus took this man's word and used it a little later Himself.

The ruler of the synagogue turned to all the people and said, "Let me preach you a sermon. You see what this fellow did. He healed this woman on the Sabbath day. That ought not to be done. Let me tell you what ought to be done."

A little later we find the Lord Jesus saying, "No, let Me tell you what ought to be done." This man was critical of Christ's work. If we are not careful, we can be critical of Christ's work. All of us have an idea about how God is to do His work.

We should be careful about trying to play God and making a decision with finality about why people are suffering.

Of course, everything should be true to Scripture, doctrinally sound. But the Lord may choose to do something that we would call totally out of the ordinary. If we are not careful, we can get in such a rut that we attempt to box God up in a way that the Holy Spirit is not at liberty to work in our lives.

This ruler of the synagogue said, "I'm going to tell You something. I saw what You did, and it is not right." Do you know what his problem was? He was the ruler of the synagogue, the man who called on people to read the Scriptures and decided who was going to lead in prayer. He was so concerned about the routine, the way everything worked, that he lost sight of God.

I know that he lost sight of God because he did not care about the healing of this woman. When a man really walks with God and knows God and sees God, God gives that man a burden to help people and rejoice when people's lives are changed by Christ.

May the Lord give us freedom and liberty to rejoice in what He is doing in the lives of people as He sets them free from the Devil's bondage.

The Lord Jesus said to this ruler, *"Thou hypocrite."* In other words, "You have a role as a religious leader, but you are just playing the role and have no genuine heart for God. You are pretending to be something that you are not, and you are a hypocrite." The woman may have been bound, but this man was blind.

This man allowed the crowd to criticize also. The Bible goes on to say that all the adversaries of Christ were ashamed. Who do you think led those adversaries? This fellow did. He had his crowd there.

This synagogue was divided. They were ashamed. I would like to think that it was the right kind of shame, but I do not believe that it was. Their hearts were not melted. They were not humbled by all of this. They were ashamed because they had no answer for Christ when He rebuked them. They could not answer Him.

THE COMPASSION OF THE SAVIOR

The Lord saw the woman. Many times in life when we are stooped low, and it seems the only place we can look is down, we may wonder if God is anywhere around. Just as the Bible says that Christ saw this woman, He sees you and me. There is never a time when we are out of God's sight.

There may be things we allow to take God out of our spiritual sight, but there is never a time when we are out of His sight. When it seems we cannot find Him, He can always find us. As Job said, *"He knoweth the way that I take."* Christ saw this woman.

The Bible says that the Lord Jesus called out to her. Can you imagine what it would be like to hear the voice of the Lord Jesus call to you and single you out?

The Lord Jesus called unto her, and the Bible says in verse thirteen, *"And he laid his hands on her:..."* This is what the ruler did not like, when the Lord actually touched her. He considered this to be work. The

Word of God says, *"...and immediately she was made straight, and glorified God."* Imagine this lady who was bent over, then she was immediately straightened up. Her posture was perfectly straight, after eighteen years of this bondage.

This ruler became angry, and the Lord said in verse fifteen, *"Thou hypocrite."* The voice of Christ was the voice of love. It was an angry voice. You may say, "What? Jesus was angry?" Yes. The Lord got angry at sin. It was certainly controlled anger, but it was a voice of love that said, *"Thou hypocrite."* The same One who embraces and pulls us to Himself is the same One who speaks against our enemies and lifts His voice against what is wrong.

If we are not careful, we can get in such a rut that we attempt to box God up in a way that the Holy Spirit is not at liberty to work in our lives.

I hope you never fall into the trap of thinking that if someone preaches hard against sin and calls sin by name, that person does not have love. It is because we do love the Lord and love people that we lift our voices against sin and what is wrong.

The Lord Jesus said in verse fifteen, *"Thou hypocrite, doth not each one of you on the sabbath loose his ox or his ass from the stall, and lead him away to watering?"* He said, "Don't you know the difference between the value of dumb animals and the value of a human being?"

In our day, many people take better care of their pets and show better care for animals than they do for people. May God convict us. The Lord said, "Don't you see that healing a woman is of greater value than watering an animal? You are a hypocrite."

The man said in verse fourteen, *"There are six days in which men ought to work."* Christ took that same word *"ought,"* and He said in verse sixteen, *"And ought not this woman, being a daughter of*

Abraham, whom Satan hath bound, lo, these eighteen years, be loosed from this bond on the sabbath day?"

The Lord said, "You are saying what ought to be done as a blind person bound in the kingdom of Satan. I am telling you what ought to be done in the work of God."

Luke 13:17 says, *"And when he had said these things, all his adversaries were ashamed: and all the people rejoiced for all the glorious things that were done by him."* I wonder if we are able to rejoice over all the glorious things that are done by Him. Sometimes we get so troubled about the mechanical part of life, how things are to work, how they should be done, that we lose sight of what is really being done.

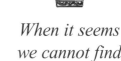

When it seems we cannot find Him, He can always find us.

The Word of God says in Luke 13:18-19, *"Then said he, Unto what is the kingdom of God like? and whereunto shall I resemble it? It is like a grain of a mustard seed, which a man took, and cast into his garden; and it grew, and waxed a great tree; and the fowls of the air lodged in the branches of it."*

This tree grew and grew, but that is not what a mustard seed is supposed to do. They knew that a grain of mustard seed did not grow into a great tree that birds of the air lodged in. The mustard plant was an herb type of plant. This was an unnatural growth.

Christ was saying that men have built a religious system that grows and grows, but it is without Christ. We see so much of this today. It is all around us, a religious system and religious ordinances without Christ. Is Christ's presence real in your life?

May God deliver us from being dead, cold, heartless, and unable to rejoice when lives are being changed. Let us be genuine.

We are to live in obedience to the Lord Jesus Christ. We do not have to apologize for that. The Lord wants His people to be holy people. We are trying to walk the straight and narrow and do what is right, but at the same time, we must keep our hearts right with God.

Let us not get puffed up with ourselves, thinking of how great we are, and how right we are, and take our eyes off God. We want to be able to rejoice over what God is doing.

The Bible says in Luke 13:17, *"And all the people rejoiced for all the glorious things that were done by him."* Rejoice now in what the Lord Jesus has done in your life and in the lives of others.

Chapter Eight

JESUS LOVED LAZARUS

 hen we look at this great story, we see a number of characters. Perhaps we could give our attention to Martha and Mary or to Lazarus. Perhaps we could give attention to the people who came to comfort them in the death of Lazarus. Perhaps we could even give attention to the messenger that was sent from the sisters to inform the Lord Jesus of the illness of Lazarus. Whoever we may identify with in the story, we must not get our eyes off the Lord Jesus.

We are looking at this mighty miracle performed by the Lord Jesus Christ in restoring Lazarus back to life, raising him from the dead. The Bible says in John 11:1-10,

> *Now a certain man was sick, named Lazarus, of Bethany, the town of Mary and her sister Martha. (It was that Mary which anointed the Lord with ointment, and wiped his feet with her hair, whose brother Lazarus was sick.) Therefore his sisters*

sent unto him, saying, Lord, behold, he whom thou lovest is sick. When Jesus heard that, he said, This sickness is not unto death, but for the glory of God, that the Son of God might be glorified thereby. Now Jesus loved Martha, and her sister, and Lazarus. When he had heard therefore that he was sick, he abode two days still in the same place where he was. Then after that saith he to his disciples, Let us go into Judæa again. His disciples say unto him, Master, the Jews of late sought to stone thee; and goest thou thither again? Jesus answered, Are there not twelve hours in the day? If any man walk in the day, he stumbleth not, because he seeth the light of this world. But if a man walk in the night, he stumbleth, because there is no light in him.

As we begin traveling through this story, we come to verse five of John chapter eleven, and we find a great truth. The Bible says, *"Jesus loved...Lazarus."* With everything else that happens in this story, let us never forget that statement. With the divine delaying, let us not forget this statement, *"Jesus loved...Lazarus."*

The Devil attempts to blind us to the goodness of God. The Bible says that *"the goodness of God leadeth thee to repentance"* (Romans 2:4). We are apt to forget that we are loved by God with an everlasting love. Just in case we do not understand what God is doing, the Lord reminds us here, "Don't fret. Don't worry. Don't ever question this truth. I love him and I love his sisters." The Bible says, *"Now Jesus loved Martha, and her sister, and Lazarus."*

When I think of the messenger that was sent to Christ and His disciples, I understand that his words were heard by our Lord. Many times in life, that is all I am and all I can be–a messenger to the Lord. Often that is all I am able to do. I should not go to the Lord to attempt to order Him around. I am not going to the Lord with some pretense. I can come boldly before the throne of grace and approach Him on His merit, not my own; on His shed blood, not anything that I have done. I lay my case before the Lord as a messenger, just as this messenger came. He presented his case to Christ. He carried this message, *"He whom thou lovest is sick."*

The messenger was saying, "Jesus, You do as You please. I know whatever You please to do will be the right thing. But I have done my part; I have brought You the message." May God help us to do our part and trust God to do His part. Our part is to carry the message to the throne of grace just as this messenger came and said, *"He whom thou lovest is sick."*

No doubt the messenger was affected by the sickness of Lazarus. No doubt Mary was affected by the sickness of Lazarus. No doubt Martha was affected by the sickness of Lazarus. No doubt neighbors were affected by the sickness of Lazarus. No doubt Lazarus was greatly affected by his own illness. But let us not forget the Lord Jesus. His heart was moved over the need of this man.

HIS LOVE

As we look at this story, think of this–*"Jesus loved...Lazarus."* As we look at Christ, I want you to consider His love. Notice where God places this statement. In the opening part of this account, we read in verses one through three,

> *Now a certain man was sick, named Lazarus, of Bethany, the town of Mary and her sister Martha. (It was that Mary which anointed the Lord with ointment, and wiped his feet with her hair, whose brother Lazarus was sick.) Therefore his sisters sent unto him, saying, Lord, behold, he whom thou lovest is sick.*

This was the message the messenger brought to Christ from the sisters of Lazarus, Mary and Martha. The message they gave the messenger was to tell the Lord Jesus, *"He whom thou lovest is sick."*

We find recorded in God's Word the words of the sisters delivered to the Savior by this chosen messenger. As we read on, the Bible says, *"When Jesus heard that, he said, This sickness is not unto death,..."* In other words, the outcome, the end product of this would not be death, *"...but for the glory of God, that the Son of God might be glorified thereby."*

In this place the Lord gives us this statement, *"Now Jesus loved Martha, and her sister, and Lazarus."* Right before verse six, God tells us that He loved them. Then in verse six He says, *"When he had heard therefore that he was sick, he abode two days still in the same place where he was."*

In the natural mind, this does not sound like love. God knows that it does not sound like love or look like love. It is not a response that we think is loving. But before God tells that Christ stayed there two days after He got this message, He says, "I want you to know I am going to delay, but My delay is a loving delay. It may not appear to you to be love, but I want you to understand without question that I do love Lazarus. I also love Mary and I love Martha. Just because I am going to stay here two days does not mean that I do not love them. I am waiting because of love." This was a delay prompted by our Lord's love for Lazarus.

I think we should say, "Lord, no matter what circumstance I am in, no matter what I am dealing with or what my loved ones are dealing with, no matter what it appears my prayers get done or do not get done, help me from this moment to the day I see Your face to never doubt that You love me and that You desire what is best for me."

I think it took greater love for the Lord Jesus to stay than it would have taken for Him to go. How can we talk about God's love in degrees? It cannot be dealt with like our love can be dealt with. No doubt Christ placed a restraint upon Himself. He wanted to go to the side of Mary and Martha at this time, but He waited. A greater miracle than healing a sick man was going to take place.

The Lord here is saying to us in very plain language, "When you do not understand exactly what I am doing, never doubt whether or not I love you."

In the Old Testament, in Isaiah 30:18, the Bible says, *"And therefore will the LORD wait, that he may be gracious unto you, and therefore will he be exalted, that he may have mercy upon you: for the LORD is a God of judgment: blessed are all they that wait for him."*

Note the opening part of verse eighteen, *"And therefore will the LORD wait,..."* Why does He wait? *"...that he may be gracious unto you."*

God has things for us that we are not able to receive. We believe we are able to receive them, and we want them at a certain time, but He waits so that we are truly able to receive more of His graciousness.

The Bible says He waits in order to be gracious to us, *"...therefore will he be exalted, that he may have mercy upon you: for the LORD is a God of judgment: blessed are all they that wait for him."* God waits in order to be gracious to us. This is a precious verse.

Notice another story about doubting whether Christ cares recorded in Mark 4:35-38,

> *And the same day, when the even was come, he saith unto them, Let us pass over unto the other side. And when they had sent away the multitude, they took him even as he was in the ship. And there were also with him other little ships. And there arose a great storm of wind, and the waves beat into the ship, so that it was now full. And he was in the hinder part of*

the ship, asleep on a pillow: and they awake him, and say unto him, Master, carest thou not that we perish?

Do we really need to ask God if He cares? Can we simply say, "God, by faith each day, help us to believe that You love us and that You have allowed this to come into our lives because You love us"?

The disciples said, *"Carest thou not that we perish?"* How could the disciples perish with Jesus Christ on board? Certainly He loved them and they could not have possibly perished. The story continues in verses thirty-nine through forty-one,

> *A greater miracle than healing a sick man was going to take place.*

And he arose, and rebuked the wind, and said unto the sea, Peace, be still. And the wind ceased, and there was a great calm. And he said unto them, Why are ye so fearful? how is it that ye have no faith? And they feared exceedingly, and said one to another, What manner of man is this, that even the wind and the sea obey him?

May God help us not to question the Lord's love for us. You may not understand all of His doings or all of His ways. You may not understand your waiting. You may not understand God's delays, but never doubt His love.

HIS LEADING

Why did the Lord wait? Note the expression in John 11:4, *"For the glory of God."* The Bible says, *"When Jesus heard that, he said, This sickness is not unto death, but for the glory of God,..."* Let us understand what God was doing. This was for the glory of God. This is why whatever we do should be done for the glory of God. We are to do all things for the glory of God, *"...that the Son of God might be glorified thereby."*

Why did Christ wait two days? Because that was the way God the Father led Him. The Lord Jesus Christ came into the world, not to do His own will, but the will of Him that sent Him.

John 6:38 says, *"For I came down from heaven, not to do mine own will, but the will of him that sent me."* One of the most amazing things in the life of Christ as we look at His earthly ministry was His humility and His yielding in obedience to the Father.

Why did Christ not go immediately back to where Lazarus was sick? Why did He wait two days? Because it was the will of the Father that He wait two days. He submitted Himself to the will of the Father.

> *God has things for us that we are not able to receive. We believe we are able to receive them, and we want them at a certain time, but He waits so that we are truly able to receive more of His graciousness.*

Christ in His earthly ministry was given to the obedience of the Father. He was in obedience to the Father for the glory of God that the Son might be glorified. Christ waited two days after He heard the message. This is the way He was led of God the Father. God the Son was led of God the Father to wait.

If we expect God's blessing, if we expect God's best in our lives, we must learn that we must also wait for the Father to lead us. We must learn by faith to trust the Father, for the heavenly Father to lead us, for the heavenly Father to show us step by step, moment by moment, what He desires for us.

The Miracles of Jesus

One of the safest things a Christian will ever do is to wait on the Lord, to be led of the Spirit of God. It may not make sense to the human mind and the natural man may rebel, but you know in your heart when there is doubt and God has not given a plain path–wait!

The messenger arrived and said to the Lord Jesus, *"He whom thou lovest is sick."* Instead of making haste and going with the messenger, the Lord waited two days because it was for the glory of God. That was how He was led. May the Lord teach us to wait upon Him.

> *If we expect God's blessing, if we expect God's best in our lives, we must learn that we must also wait for the Father to lead us.*

I believe in God's timing. God will give us everything He desires for our lives. The hard thing is not God providing; the hard thing is our waiting on the Lord to provide.

Nothing is difficult for God. We use terms like "difficult" and "hard" and "hard cases" and "being between a rock and a hard place." The Lord does not use that kind of language. He is never between a rock and a hard place. There is nothing difficult for God. There are no hard cases. There is nothing impossible with God.

The problem is not with God; the problem is our lack of waiting on God and being led of God. We may do something quickly, and we might see the glory in it; but if we had waited on God to come through and provide, God could have received great glory. He moves and works, and we praise Him and say that it could not have been done if the Lord had not done it.

HIS LIFE

In John chapter eleven, the Lord Jesus makes some powerful statements. In verse seven the Bible says, *"Then after that saith he to his disciples, Let us go into Judæa again."*

Notice back in John 10:39 the Bible says, *"Therefore they sought again to take him: but he escaped out of their hand."* The Jews were outraged at Christ; they wanted to put Him to death; they wanted to destroy Him. The Bible says He told His disciples, *"Let us go into Judæa again."*

His disciples said unto Him, *"Master, the Jews of late sought to stone thee; and goest thou thither again?"* In other words, "You are going to go right back to where they began to stone You?" And the Lord answered, *"Are there not twelve hours in the day? If any man walk in the day, he stumbleth not, because he seeth the light of this world."*

What does this mean? Let us look back in John chapter seven and verse thirty. The Bible says, *"Then they sought to take him: but no man laid hands on him, because his hour was not yet come."*

> *One of the safest things a Christian will ever do is to wait on the Lord, to be led of the Spirit of God.*

The Lord Jesus has taught us here that as far as His life is concerned and the time of His death is concerned, nothing could bring that about because it all had to go through God the Father's hands to get to Him. God was not going to allow it until the time was perfect. In other words, not a hair of His head could be harmed until it was in God's timing for sinners to take Him and crucify Him.

The Lord Jesus answered His disciples in John 11:9, *"Are there not twelve hours in the day?..."* In other words, let us talk about life like a day.

"...If any man walk in the day, he stumbleth not, because he seeth the light of this world." In other words, there are daylight hours, and the darkness does not come until the daylight hours are finished. When the daylight hours are finished, then the darkness is going to come. One cannot hold it back. If you walk in the light in the daylight and the sunshine, you do not stumble because you are walking in the light.

> *The hard thing is not God providing; the hard thing is our waiting on the Lord to provide.*

The light that we walk in is spiritual light; the fellowship we have is fellowship with Christ. The day we live is not a twelve-hour day; it is the span of life God has allotted to us. We do not know how long it is.

We look back and say, "Christ is going to be on earth thirty-three and a half years and then He is going to give Himself into the hands of angry sinners and they are going to take Him to Calvary and crucify Him, but not until it is God's time for it to happen. It is not going to happen until then."

Christ said, "It is not going to happen. Do not worry and fret about Me being prematurely put to death."

Is it possible that we could take that same principle and say, "God has given me a span of life. As I seek to obey Him and walk in the light knowing that God has an assignment for me, I do not need to worry and fret about what is going to happen to me. I am going to be cautious. I am going to be careful. But I am not going to leave here until God is finished with me. When God is finished with me, I am going to leave here."

My life has a daylight hour or hours. When the daylight hours are finished, that is it. It might be three score and ten; it may not be. But God has a life for me to live and when He is finished with it, it is finished and I will go home to be with Him.

There is something we must realize–we have an allotted time, and it will some day come to an end. Nothing we can do will keep that from happening. We do not need to worry and fret every day about dying because as we obey God, those things that can take our lives are not going to come to us without coming through God's hands first. As we walk in the light and fellowship with Him, we do not worry and fret about dying because God is going to keep us alive until He is finished with us.

I believe it is my business not to worry and fret about disease or death; it is my business to follow after Christ and trust in Him, to fellowship with Him, to walk in the light He gives me, to know that I have an allotted time on this earth, and to make the most of it because it will come to an end just as surely as the life of Christ came to an end as far as His earthly ministry was concerned.

What I want to do is everything God has for me in this time He has allotted to me. What do you want to do with your life?

We need to remember that the Lord Jesus loved Lazarus, and He loves us. Maybe you do not know what is going on in your life; maybe you do not understand it all. You may ask, "Why did this happen?" Wait on the Lord. Never doubt that the Lord Jesus loves you just as He loved Lazarus.

Chapter Nine

JESUS WEPT

or the most part, we associate weeping with people who are brokenhearted. In the miracle we are considering, we see our Lord in tears. We are taking a long look at this particular miracle when the Lord Jesus restored Lazarus back to life. The Bible says in John 11:25-37,

Jesus said unto her, I am the resurrection, and the life: he that believeth in me, though he were dead, yet shall he live: and whosoever liveth and believeth in me shall never die. Believest thou this? She saith unto him, Yea, Lord: I believe that thou art the Christ, the Son of God, which should come into the world. And when she had so said, she went her way, and called Mary her sister secretly, saying, The Master is come, and calleth for thee. As soon as she heard that, she arose quickly, and came unto him. Now Jesus was not yet

come into the town, but was in that place where Martha met him. The Jews then which were with her in the house, and comforted her, when they saw Mary, that she rose up hastily and went out, followed her, saying, She goeth unto the grave to weep there. Then when Mary was come where Jesus was, and saw him, she fell down at his feet, saying unto him, Lord, if thou hadst been here, my brother had not died. When Jesus therefore saw her weeping, and the Jews also weeping which came with her, he groaned in the spirit, and was troubled, and said, Where have ye laid him? They said unto him, Lord, come and see. Jesus wept. Then said the Jews, Behold how he loved him! And some of them said, Could not this man, which opened the eyes of the blind, have caused that even this man should not have died?

I want to call your attention to two powerful words in verse thirty-five, this shortest verse in God's Word in our English Bible. It simply says, *"Jesus wept."*

When the Lord Jesus came near Bethany in verse twenty-one, Martha came to Him and said, *"Lord, if thou hadst been here, my brother had not died."* When Martha ran to the house and found Mary her sister and said, *"The Master is come, and calleth for thee,"* Mary left her place and ran to Christ and said the same thing, *"Lord, if thou hadst been here, my brother had not died."*

As our Lord moved onto this scene, the Jews said that Mary went to the grave to weep. When the Lord Jesus came in verse thirty-three, the Bible says He saw her weeping. He also saw the Jews weeping. Then the Word of God says, *"Jesus wept."*

Here we see a picture of God in tears. There is no way for us to deal with all that this expression *"Jesus wept"* means, but it does serve as a window through which we can view certain things about our Lord that should help us to love Him more and to serve Him more faithfully.

Three times in God's Word the Bible tells us of Jesus Christ weeping. In Luke chapter nineteen the Bible tells us of Christ weeping over Jerusalem. The Word of God says in Luke 19:41-42, *"And when he was come near, he beheld the city, and wept over it, saying, If thou hadst known, even thou, at least in this thy day, the things which belong unto thy peace! but now they are hid from thine eyes."*

Notice the little word *"if"* in verse forty-two. Opportunity came and was gone. Because Christ knew what they had missed and knew what was coming to them, the Bible says He wept over the city.

Imagine standing on the side of the Mount of Olives with the city of Jerusalem in view. In your mind, see the Son of God standing there and see His body physically moving as He weeps, as He sheds tears, as He is moved with compassion upon that city because He knows what they have rejected and what is coming to them. Here again we see our God in tears.

In Hebrews 5:7 the Bible says, *"Who in the days of his flesh, when he had offered up prayers and supplications with strong crying and tears unto him that was able to save him from death, and was heard in that he feared."* He wept here. I believe that Hebrews chapter five and verse seven refers back to the Garden of Gethsemane as Christ shed tears over a lost world. Our weeping Savior, our God in tears, should stir our hearts to think that He loves us so.

As we return to this scene in John chapter eleven, I want you to notice some things. If we move up close beside this verse and use it as a window through which to view our Savior, there are things this verse tells us about our Savior.

JESUS WEPT BECAUSE OF WHAT SIN HAD DONE TO THE WHOLE WORLD

The Bible says, *"Jesus wept."* He wept because of what sin had done to the whole world. He approached a death scene here. Hearts were filled with sorrow, separation, brokenness, and earthly finality. A brother they loved was gone from them. Beyond that, Christ saw what caused all of this.

> *There is no way for us to deal with all that this expression "Jesus wept" means, but it does serve as a window through which we can view certain things about our Lord that should help us to love Him more and to serve Him more faithfully.*

In Romans 5:12 the Bible says, *"Wherefore, as by one man sin entered into the world, and death by sin; and so death passed upon all men, for that all have sinned."*

In Romans chapter five, God takes us all the way back to the Garden of Eden. In chapter three of Genesis, the serpent came and was used of the Devil as a channel for the message of Satan to get to Adam and Eve. They sinned against God. They broke God's Law. They transgressed. Sin entered into the blood stream of all humanity. What a scene in Genesis chapter three when all the world was touched, wrecked, and ruined by sin.

Christ stood in Bethany near the tomb of Lazarus among weeping people whose hearts were broken. The Lord Jesus knew in His heart that sin had brought all the heartache and sorrow to the world. He wept.

We live in a world of heartache and sorrow brought on by sin.

Notice in John 11:32-33, *"Then when Mary was come where Jesus was, and saw him, she fell down at his feet."* That was her place–at His feet. Mary said, *"Lord, if thou hadst been here, my brother had not died. When Jesus therefore saw her weeping, and the Jews also weeping which came with her, he groaned...."* This is a word expressing deep emotion. I am told by the commentators that the word *"groaned"* even expresses indignation. Some men have interpreted the verse to even express anger. Christ moved Himself with indignation. *"He groaned in the spirit, and was troubled."*

I do not think Christ's groaning and His troubling had to do with the death of Lazarus and the tears of Mary, Martha, and the Jews as much as it had to do with the whole situation. He thought of what sin had done to the human race, to the world that God made. This moved Christ to tears.

When we see the world in which we live, we think of the wreck that sin has made of it and of mankind, separating us from God, the earth groaning beneath the sin curse. As we look through this window of tears, we see that Christ wept for what sin had done to the world.

JESUS WEPT BECAUSE HE WAS BRINGING SOMEONE HE LOVED BACK TO SUCH A WORLD

We know in this story that Christ was going to bring Lazarus back. Later, we will come to the portion of Scripture where He called him forth by name. I believe that we look through this window of His tears and see that He wept because He was bringing someone He loved back to such a world.

If we could see beyond the veil as God sees beyond the veil, there would be nothing of this world that we would desire. Oh, that God would strengthen us, encourage us, speak to us, and deal with us so that we might see heaven more as Christ sees it–being with Him.

I am concerned about where heaven is. I am concerned about what is there. I am concerned about its beauty, glory, and splendor and all the saints who are there. But I am rejoicing more and more in this great truth–to be absent from the body is to be present with the Lord. Heaven is what waits at the end of the Christian life. Hell is what waits at the end of a Christless life.

In John chapter eleven, Lazarus had died. He had left this world of sorrow, heartache, and pain. The Lord was going to restore him back to life. This mighty miracle would be witnessed by so many. Christ would call him back to life and back to earth. Knowing what our Lord knows about what lies beyond the grave for believers, it is no wonder Christ wept to bring him back here, to leave all that is there.

If we could see beyond the veil as God sees beyond the veil, there would be nothing of this world that we would desire.

It strengthens me, it encourages me to think of what God has in store beyond this life for those of us who know Him and love Him. Friends, if heaven is not real, let us just give up altogether. We are of all men most miserable if our Lord has not gone through the grave and resurrected bodily from the dead. We have no hope, no future. We have absolutely nothing if Christ be not risen. But if He truly did conquer death, hell, and the grave and He does hold the keys in His hands, then think what splendor and glory and beauty God has for us in the heaven He has prepared for us. No wonder the Lord Jesus wept to bring Lazarus back to a world such as this. This mighty miracle gives witness to the power of the Lord Jesus. It testifies to the truth that He is who He says He is.

JESUS WEPT FOR THOSE
WHO WERE WEEPING

The sisters of Lazarus were weeping. The Jew were weeping. Christ was weeping. He was in the company of tears and He wept. Let us read it again. The Bible says in verse thirty-three, *"When Jesus therefore saw her weeping, and the Jews also weeping which came with her, he groaned in the spirit, and was troubled, and said, Where have ye laid him? They said unto him, Lord, come and see."*

This is so very precious. The Lord knew exactly where they had laid Lazarus. He knows all things. He is fully God; surely He knew exactly where Lazarus was. But what did He desire? He wanted to be invited to the grave site. He wanted them to desire Him to be there. So He asked them, *"Where have ye laid him?"*

The Lord knows all about us. He knew all about us before we were ever born. Why does He wait at our heart's door? Why does He bid us by His Holy Spirit with questions? Why is it that He wants us to pray when He is always praying for us and knows the outcome of everything? It is because He wants to be invited to our need.

Do you wish for Him to come to your aid? How far away is Christ? In your pain and what you are dealing with, how far away is He now? How far away is He at this moment? What does He desire to do?

When my children hurt, not just when they were little but even now, I want to be by their side. I want them to feel my touch. I want them to hear my voice. I want them to know that I am with them. Though limited I may be as just another human being, whatever I can do, I want to do. When our children hurt, we hurt with them. This is how Christ feels.

I want you to consider a great truth from God's Word. In I Peter 2:24-25 the Bible says, *"Who his own self bare our sins in his own body on the tree, that we, being dead to sins, should live unto righteousness: by whose stripes ye were healed. For ye were as sheep going astray; but are now returned unto the Shepherd and Bishop of your souls."*

There is a little word in verse twenty-four I want you to note. It is the word *"bare."* Here the word *"bare"* means "to lift up and carry away into God's eternal forgetfulness."

Christ bares our sins. He lifts them up and carries them away into God's eternal forgetfulness. They shall never be remembered against us again. As the scapegoat on the day of atonement going into the

But if He truly did conquer death, hell, and the grave and He does hold the keys in His hands, then think what splendor and glory and beauty God has for us in the heaven He has prepared for us.

wilderness, carrying our sins away, the Bible says that Jesus Christ bares our sins and lifts them up, carries them away into God's eternal forgetfulness, never to be remembered again. Therefore, He sees me justified–just as if I had never even been a sinner. My sins are gone.

In the Gospel according to Matthew, the Bible tells of the healing of Peter's mother-in-law. In chapter eight and verse fourteen, Christ had come into Peter's house. The Bible says in verses fourteen through seventeen,

And when Jesus was come into Peter's house, he saw his wife's mother laid, and sick of a fever. And he touched her hand, and the fever left her: and she arose, and ministered unto them. When the even was come, they brought unto him many that were possessed with devils: and he cast out the spirits with his word, and healed all that were sick: that it might be fulfilled which was spoken by Esaias

*the prophet, saying, Himself took our infirmities, and
bare our sicknesses.*

The word *"bare"* is used again. Here the word *"bare"* means "to
get under the load in love." There are things we are going to go
through in this life that are inescapable. I do not want to go through
them. As a matter of fact, I want God to deal with them the same way
He deals with my sins. I want Him to take them and lift them up and
carry them away into His eternal forgetfulness. I want God to bare all
my sorrows, all my troubles, all my griefs, and all my heartaches. I
want God to do all that for me just as He deals with my sin.

There are some people who teach that Christ does this with all of
our sicknesses and all our diseases, but they do not understand the
Bible. They cause great harm to come upon people by not
understanding the Scriptures. Isaiah chapter fifty-three is quoted in
Matthew chapter eight. We read in this chapter about what Christ did
with our sin. *"All we like sheep have gone astray; we have turned
every one to his own way; and the LORD hath laid on him the iniquity
of us all."* As the iniquity of us all was laid on Him, He carried that
sin away forever into God's eternal forgetfulness. But He does
something clsc.

In addition to bearing our sins away into God's forgetfulness, He
also bares our griefs and our sorrows. He does not carry them away,
but He gets under the load in love. This is what we are dealing with
when we come to Isaiah 53:3-4,

> *He is despised and rejected of men; a man of
> sorrows, and acquainted with grief: and we hid as it
> were our faces from him; he was despised, and we
> esteemed him not. Surely he hath borne our griefs,
> and carried our sorrows: yet we did esteem him
> stricken, smitten of God, and afflicted.*

What does this mean? It means that life here in this sin-cursed world is going to be a life with some heartache, sorrow, suffering, and disappointment. My sins are gone eternally, forever, in the sea of God's forgetfulness. What about my griefs and sorrows? I say to you that Lazarus was restored to life but would die again. And when he died the second time, just as Jesus came in that day in bodily presence He would come to Lazarus' loved ones in the Person of the Holy Spirit to bare their griefs with them, to get under their load in love and help them through.

If you are looking for a life where there is no sorrow, no grief, no heartache, no disappointment, it is impossible to find. I have tried to make that kind of world for people I love. I have tried to guard them and protect them just as you have tried to guard and protect people you love. You have tried to keep everything that hurts from them, just as I have tried to keep everything that hurts from people I love. You have tried to head off everything that would trouble them and cause any grief or sorrow, just as anyone who loves people tries to head off anything that causes grief or sorrow. But we cannot stop it all. It does not work that way.

Someone may say, "Well, we have heaven to look forward to because our sins are forgiven and the Lord has lifted our sins up and carried them away into God's eternal forgetfulness." That is great! It is greater than great; it is wonderful, more wonderful than I can speak of. But that is not all. He comes to us in our time of suffering and sorrow and comes under it with us and bares it in love and enables us to live through what we cannot escape. His grace is sufficient because He is sufficient.

The Bible says, *"Surely he hath borne our griefs, and carried our sorrows: yet we did esteem him stricken, smitten of God, and afflicted."* The Jews came. They knew Mary and Martha and Lazarus. They came to Mary and Martha and tried to comfort them. These two sisters said that if Christ had been there, this would have

never happened. They knew He could have prevented death. They were going to learn that He could raise someone from the dead who had been dead four days. Their faith was going to be increased.

When the Lord Jesus came on the scene and death had already taken place, the tears were already being shed. The grief was already present and He said, "Let me get in there and get under this with you, and weep with you, and share your sorrow, and bare your grief and your suffering."

You may say, "Lord, would You get rid of all my trouble, take away every heartache and every disease, spare me from every pain, and not let anything that would hurt touch anyone I love or touch me?" That is impossible.

Christ says, "I'll tell you what I'll do. Just as I came to that weeping group at Bethany, I will come to you and I will be with you. I will see you through."

> *He comes to us in our time of suffering and sorrow and comes under it with us and bares it in love and enables us to live through what we cannot escape. His grace is sufficient because He is sufficient.*

"Jesus wept." Right now, Christ is closer to you than the next breath you breathe. God in tears goes through every trial with you. What a Savior!

Chapter Ten

LAZARUS, COME FORTH

We continue to look at this wonderful miracle when Christ raised Lazarus from the dead, restoring him back to life. Our Lord had returned with His disciples to the little village of Bethany. As He approached Bethany, He was greeted by Martha, the sister of Lazarus. She said, *"Lord, if thou hadst been here, my brother had not died."* Christ was greeted by Mary, the other sister of Lazarus, with the same response. The Bible says in John 11:38-44,

> *Jesus therefore again groaning in himself cometh to the grave. It was a cave, and a stone lay upon it. Jesus said, Take ye away the stone. Martha, the sister of him that was dead, saith unto him, Lord, by this time he stinketh: for he hath been dead four days. Jesus saith unto her, Said I not unto thee, that, if thou wouldest believe, thou shouldest see the glory of God? Then they took away the stone from the place where the dead was laid. And*

> *Jesus lifted up his eyes, and said, Father, I thank thee*
> *that thou hast heard me. And I knew that thou hearest*
> *me always: but because of the people which stand by*
> *I said it, that they may believe that thou hast sent me.*
> *And when he thus had spoken, he cried with a loud*
> *voice, Lazarus, come forth. And he that was dead*
> *came forth, bound hand and foot with graveclothes:*
> *and his face was bound about with a napkin. Jesus*
> *saith unto them, Loose him, and let him go.*

Note the expression that our Lord used when He raised this man from the dead. In verse forty-three the Bible says, *"Lazarus, come forth."* The voice of God pierced across every border from the living to the dead. Lazarus heard the voice of the Lord Jesus, calling his name, and he came back to life in this world. Many stood by witnessing this miraculous event as it took place.

What does all this mean for us? I think there are some things we need to understand about life and death, things that God can use in dealing with us. In Genesis chapter two, the Bible gives us a summation of God's creation of Adam and Eve. In this passage, we learn how death entered into this world. The Word of God says in Genesis 2:8-17,

> *And the* LORD *God planted a garden eastward in*
> *Eden; and there he put the man whom he had formed.*
> *And out of the ground made the* LORD *God to grow*
> *every tree that is pleasant to the sight, and good for*
> *food; the tree of life also in the midst of the garden,*
> *and the tree of knowledge of good and evil. And a*
> *river went out of Eden to water the garden; and from*
> *thence it was parted, and became into four heads.*
> *The name of the first is Pison: that is it which*
> *compasseth the whole land of Havilah, where there is*
> *gold; and the gold of that land is good: there is*

*bdellium and the onyx stone. And the name of the
second river is Gihon: the same is it that compasseth
the whole land of Ethiopia. And the name of the third
river is Hiddekel: that is it which goeth toward the
east of Assyria. And the fourth river is Euphrates. And
the* LORD *God took the man, and put him into the
garden of Eden to dress it and to keep it. And the*
LORD *God commanded the man, saying, Of every
tree of the garden thou mayest freely eat: but of the
tree of the knowledge of good and evil, thou shalt not
eat of it: for in the day that thou eatest thereof thou
shalt surely die.*

God did not want them to die, but He said, "If you break My law, you will bring death into your own lives and death will enter into the bloodstream of all humanity."

We know that Adam and Eve did disobey God, and just as surely as God said it, they died. Death came upon their lives and they were separated from God.

God killed an innocent animal. The innocent blood was shed for the guilty, and a principle was established. This type was fulfilled in Jesus Christ. He is the Lamb of God *"slain from the foundation of the world,"* who came and shed His precious blood to take away our sin. The only way to be delivered from the eternal death we deserve as sinners is to ask God to forgive our sin and trust Jesus Christ as Savior.

As we consider this story in John chapter eleven, we see that Christ groaned in His spirit. The Bible says in John 11:38, *"Jesus therefore again groaning in himself cometh to the grave. It was a cave, and a stone lay upon it."* Notice in verse thirty-three the Bible says, *"When Jesus therefore saw her weeping, and the Jews also weeping which came with her, he groaned in the spirit, and was troubled."*

As we look at this chapter, and in particular this scene, we see Christ outwardly weeping, inwardly deeply moved and groaning in His spirit.

What moves the Son of God to such emotion? Why these tears and inward groaning? Because He sees the devastation that sin has brought to the human race and the death that is brought to all of us.

When we suffer, the Lord's heart is moved. Beyond this veil of tears, He has more for us than this life of sorrow. God has something wonderful in store for those of us who know Him and love Him. It is more wonderful than we could ever imagine.

THE PROTEST OF MARTHA

As we look at this part of the story, notice the protest of Martha. When the Lord Jesus came upon this scene, He was walking to the grave site. Lazarus' dead body had been placed into a cave.

On many occasions, as I have traveled in the Holy Land, I have been in the cave that is supposedly the tomb of Lazarus. I have gone down the stairway under the surface of the earth. On every occasion I have read John chapter eleven. I have thought, while I was deep down inside the cave, about the body of Lazarus. I have thought about him hearing the voice of the Son of God, his spirit returning to his body, and his body coming out of there.

In my mind, I have gone back to Bethany and I have imagined our Lord standing there weeping and groaning, moving on that scene to bring about a mighty miracle. But it was under protest.

The Bible says in verse thirty-nine, *"Jesus said, Take ye away the stone. Martha, the sister of him that was dead, saith unto him, Lord, by this time he stinketh: for he hath been dead four days."* Martha was protesting. She was saying, "There is no use now. If You had gotten here when Lazarus was alive, no matter how sick he was, You could have healed him. If You had gotten here immediately after he died, just like You raised the widow's son or the little girl in the house of Jairus in Capernaum, You could have brought him back. But not now. He has been dead four days. When that stone is moved, we are all going to smell the stench of his decaying body."

Martha had drawn a line, like all of us draw lines, to show how far we think God can go in His wonderful work. The Lord wants us to move the line, get it out of the way, and trust Him for all things. What can you believe God for?

The Lord wants to be glorified in our lives. Verse forty says, *"Jesus saith unto her, Said I not unto thee, that, if thou wouldest believe, thou shouldest see the glory of God?"* In other words, "If God is going to be glorified, if He is going to get the great glory that He deserves, then we have to deal with your protest, your unbelief, your lack of faith."

This same principle is true for our lives. If God is going to get the glory that He deserves, then we must deal with our protest, our lack of faith, our unbelief. The Lord cannot get the glory He deserves until we are willing to trust Him.

I praise God that He accepts our weak, anemic faith. I can remember a lady coming to my pastor years ago when I was just starting out as a young preacher. The lady said, "Brother Hagen, I don't have enough faith to get anything done. I don't have enough faith to believe God for anything." In his colloquial way of saying it, he said, "Have you got a teaspoon full?" He was speaking to a country lady. She said, "Well, I think I can get that much faith." He said, "God will take you on that." Beloved, believe God where you are. Ask for faith and more faith.

In our believing, there is always the element of unbelief, but we should desire to have great faith in God. As we think about what we must deal with, let us remember that faith is defined for us in Hebrews 12:2 as *"Looking unto Jesus."* Faith is looking away unto the Lord Jesus. When we are troubled over things that seem insurmountable, we must look away unto Jesus Christ.

When we are bothered by someone who is a snag to our faith, we must look away unto the Lord Jesus. When we seem to be overcome by something and we say, "I don't know about this," we must simply look away unto the Lord Jesus. The protest of Martha was one of unbelief. We must deal with the unbelief in our own lives. All of us are guilty of this type of protest.

THE PRAYER OF THE LORD JESUS

The Bible says in John 11:41-42,

> *Then they took away the stone from the place where the dead was laid. And Jesus lifted up his eyes, and said, Father, I thank thee that thou hast heard me. And I knew that thou hearest me always: but because of the people which stand by I said it, that they may believe that thou hast sent me.*

This was the prayer of the Lord Jesus. We need to pay close attention to our Lord's prayers. You may find many things in this prayer, but I am going to mention only two. First, He was praying for God the Father to be glorified.

Examine your own prayer life. If your prayers were to be answered, who would be glorified? Would you be glorified and exalted? Would people say, "What a magnificent human being, what a mind, what a thought, what an administrator, what a leader!"

If the things we wish for, hope for, and pray for were to come to pass, who would be glorified? God is going to work in our lives so if our prayers are truly prayers to Him and He answers them, they will be answered in a way that brings glory to Him.

I believe this has something to do with the Lord Jesus delaying His coming when He knew the severity of Lazarus' condition. Finally, He had to plainly say to His disciples, *"Lazarus is dead."* He waited until Lazarus had died to return.

The Lord Jesus prayed so that the people could hear Him talking to God the Father, and He prayed that what was done would bring glory to the Lord. I believe the Lord waits sometimes until we are in an impossible situation, at least as far as we are concerned, so that when God does hear and answers our prayer, He is glorified.

The second thing that was so powerful about this prayer was that Christ and the Father agreed in prayer. There was communion; there was agreement. He was praying in the will of God the Father.

Often we get the idea that prayer is trying to convince God to do something He does not want to do. It is as though we are begging and pleading with God to change His mind and to do something He simply does not want to do. If we succeed in prayer, we have the idea that we finally get God to come around to our way of thinking. We say, "Lord, listen up. I'm trying to convince You of something. I know You are not really in on this, but I want You to get in on it." This is not the way to pray. Prayer is not trying to get God to come around to our way of thinking; prayer is God working in our hearts until we come around to His way of thinking.

Martha had drawn a line, like all of us draw lines to show how far we think God can go in His wonderful work. The Lord wants us to move the line, get it out of the way, and trust Him for all things.

What does this mean in our day-to-day lives? It means that when we know God's will, we have every right to pray and trust God to accomplish His will. We must ask, "Is this what God wants? Will the Lord be glorified in it?"

If what we are doing is what God wants, if we are confident in our hearts that it is the will of God, then we have every right to approach the throne of grace. We can come boldly before our Savior in His merit, not our own, and ask our Father to do His will and to trust Him for it. We must pray in the will of God and ask in the name of the Lord Jesus Christ. Much time must be spent with the Lord and His Word to determine His will.

> *Faith is defined for us in Hebrews 12:2 as "Looking unto Jesus."*

When our Lord lifted up His voice to pray, He called on the Lord to bring glory to God the heavenly Father and prayed in the will of God the Father. Let us pray as the Lord Jesus prayed.

THE POWER OF GOD'S WORD

The Bible clearly says that Lazarus had been dead four days, and Christ cried with a loud voice, *"Lazarus, come forth."*

You may ask, "Why did He cry out with a loud voice?" Christ did not want to murmur. He wanted everyone standing by to know exactly what He said and exactly whose name He called.

The dead could have heard His whisper as easily as His loud voice. Those people standing by might have been thinking that the Lord Jesus had lost His mind. We read it with faith believing, but I want you to put yourself there next to that grave as He said, *"Lazarus, come forth."* They might have been saying, "Is there anyone who believes that a man can speak beyond that tomb into another world and someone who has been dead four days can actually hear his voice and obey?"

But something happened. There stood Lazarus, wrapped in grave clothes. Christ said, *"Loose him, and let him go."* In other words, "Take those clothes off him. I don't want you to have any doubt about who this is. This is not an impostor we hid in that tomb. This is the man you buried four days ago. You are going to see that this is the same man who is the brother of these two women who have been weeping over his death. He is Lazarus. Take those grave clothes off and let us see him." These people witnessed the power of the Word of God.

> *God is going to work in our lives so if our prayers are truly prayers to Him and He answers them, they will be answered in a way that brings glory to Him.*

A man was dead four days, and he heard the voice of the Son of God saying, *"Lazarus, come forth."* Think of the decaying process that had been taking place in his body for the past four days. It was all reversed and life came again. He came back into that dead body from beyond death's door, reunited with that body, and walked to the opening of that grave. He stood there and was loosed and restored back to life to live with his sisters. What a demonstration of the power of the Word of God!

You may say, "That is wonderful." Yes, it is wonderful, but think of this. I was not dead four days; I was dead in my sin for thirteen and a half years when I heard His voice. As a young teenage boy, I heard the gospel and came to Christ for salvation. By His Word, He convicted me of my sin and I asked Him to forgive me. I trusted Him as my Savior, and He came to live in me forever. He saved my lost soul.

I did not hear His voice audibly like these people heard Him call the name of Lazarus. I did not hear His voice audibly like Lazarus heard His voice. But I know God spoke to me, and I asked Him to forgive my sin. I know I trusted Him as my Savior. He came to live in me, and I know I have been redeemed.

I was dead in my trespasses and sins, but I have been made alive spiritually in the Lord Jesus Christ. Do you know that you have trusted Him?

Chapter Eleven

WHERE ARE THE NINE?

 s we consider the miracle of the healing of the ten lepers, we learn from God's Word that Jesus Christ was going to Jerusalem to bleed and die for our sins. The fact that Christ came to earth should be enough to humble all of us. He came to earth to die on Calvary. If you do not understand what the cross of Jesus Christ is all about, I want you to understand that He went to the cross to bear the sins of the whole world, to bleed and die for our sins. He was buried and He rose from the dead.

You may believe this story, but it is not good news for you until you know there is bad news. The bad news is that we are all sinners, and we all owe a sin debt. The payment of our sin is death and hell. Jesus Christ paid our debt for us so that we would not have to pay it. If you ask the Lord Jesus to forgive your sin and by faith receive Him as your Savior, He promised that He would hear your prayer, forgive your sin, and be your Savior.

The Miracles of Jesus

As Christ was going to Jerusalem to die, the Bible says in Luke 17:11-19,

> *And it came to pass, as he went to Jerusalem, that he passed through the midst of Samaria and Galilee. And as he entered into a certain village, there met him ten men that were lepers, which stood afar off: and they lifted up their voices, and said, Jesus, Master, have mercy on us. And when he saw them, he said unto them, Go shew yourselves unto the priests. And it came to pass, that, as they went, they were cleansed. And one of them, when he saw that he was healed, turned back, and with a loud voice glorified God, and fell down on his face at his feet, giving him thanks: and he was a Samaritan. And Jesus answering said, Were there not ten cleansed? but where are the nine? There are not found that returned to give glory to God, save this stranger. And he said unto him, Arise, go thy way: thy faith hath made thee whole.*

Look closely at the question Christ asked in verse seventeen, *"Where are the nine?"* Immediately we think He was speaking only of the nine lepers who were cleansed and did not return to give Him thanks. But the truth is, He was speaking about all of us who have forgotten to be grateful to God. Christ asked, *"Where are the nine?"* Are we truly grateful to God for what He has done for us?

This seems like such a simple story. It is one of those Bible stories we read and think it needs little or no explanation. Christ was traveling through Galilee and Samaria, along the border of these areas. The people of Samaria were called Samaritans. The Jews had great prejudice against the Samaritans and because of this had nothing to do with them.

As Christ traveled along this border area, He came to a little village. Coming out of that village were ten lepers in a group. They would not get near Him, but from afar they cried out, *"Jesus, Master, have mercy on us."*

In our country, we do not know much about lepers or leprosy. But in some parts of the world, people still deal with this disease. These leprous men were believed to be terrible sinners because in the minds of the leaders of their land, leprosy was a result of their awful sin.

Here they were, bound together by this common misery, leprosy, crying out to Christ. The Lord Jesus said, *"Go shew yourselves unto the priests."* The Bible says as they moved in that direction, they were cleansed.

Can you imagine how they felt when they looked at their bodies and saw that they were cleansed? The Bible says that one of these men returned to Christ. He was a Samaritan. We assume from this that the others were Jews. This is not some sort of slanderous statement toward Jews because they did not return, but the Bible says that the Samaritan was the one that returned.

Perhaps when these men were all healed, the leprosy was no longer something that bound them together, and they returned to their natural prejudice. The one man made his way to Christ, fell on his face at the feet of the Lord Jesus, and with a loud voice gave glory to God. Our Lord made a powerful statement here. He said to the man in verse nineteen, *"Arise, go thy way: thy faith hath made thee whole."* All ten of the lepers were healed of their physical malady, but only one came to know the Lord Jesus as his personal Savior. Only one was made *"whole."*

If all that had happened to them was the healing from leprosy, then they would have all died and gone to hell according to what the Bible says. There is only one way to heaven. The only way to heaven is the way that Christ has made. He said, *"I am the way, the truth, and the life: no man cometh unto the Father, but by me"* (John 14:6).

You may say, "I don't believe that." I can respect your right to have an opinion, but whether you believe it or not does not change the truth. The truth is, Jesus Christ, God's Son, came to this earth, lived a sinless life, and went to the cross. He did not pay His own debt, He paid our debt. He owed no debt to sin. He bore our sins in His own body and satisfied the holiness of God that demanded that sin must be paid for. Christ paid that debt, was buried, and rose from the grave, alive forevermore.

> *All ten of the lepers were healed of their physical malady, but only one came to know the Lord Jesus as his personal Savior. Only one was made "whole."*

If we ask Him to forgive our sin, trusting in what He did on the cross, He has promised to forgive our sin and come to live in us and give us a home in heaven.

To one of those ten lepers, the Samaritan, the Lord said, *"Thy faith hath made thee whole."* He was saying, "Not only are you healed, not only are you cleansed, but you are made whole. You are a new man, not just on the outside, but on the inside too. The Lord has come to live in you."

What great lessons do we learn from this miracle? They have to do with thankfulness. The Bible warns us of things that we are to be aware of in the last days. The warning was given to the apostle Paul to pen under the inspiration of the Spirit of God in II Timothy chapter three. One of those things is an unthankful spirit. The Bible says in II Timothy 3:1-2, *"This know also, that in the last days perilous times shall come. For men shall be lovers of their own selves, covetous, boasters, proud, blasphemers, disobedient to parents, unthankful, unholy."*

We are living in a time of ingratitude. It is as though worldwide, people have the idea that everything is owed to them. The truth is, there is a spirit of ingratitude in all of us. We are warned against it. We can glean some things from this miracle that will help us to be more grateful.

THE CAUSE OF GRATITUDE

Some people are terribly unhappy because they have attached their gratitude to the wrong things. When we start thinking about what we are grateful for, we need to get to the very heart of the cause of gratitude and never forget it.

For example, I am grateful for the measure of health I enjoy. However, it is not always God's will for people to be well. It is not always God's will for people to be strong. Does that shock you?

The apostle Paul, giving a testimony in II Corinthians 12:7-9, penned these words,

> *And lest I should be exalted above measure through the abundance of the revelations, there was given to me a thorn in the flesh, the messenger of Satan to buffet me, lest I should be exalted above measure. For this thing I besought the Lord thrice, that it might depart from me. And he said unto me, My grace is sufficient for thee: for my strength is made perfect in weakness. Most gladly therefore will I rather glory in my infirmities, that the power of Christ may rest upon me.*

Paul said, "Take it away." But God said to him, *"My grace is sufficient for thee."* In other words, the Lord said, "Paul, you are going to be a sick man. You are going to deal with sickness."

151

If you are grateful only because you are healthy, then when you are not feeling well, you will not be grateful. Paul said, *"My strength is made perfect in weakness."* If the only reason you have for being grateful is being strong, then when you are not strong, you will not be grateful.

I hear people say, "I can't serve God unless I am completely well and very strong." I do not know of anyone who ever served the Lord more than the apostle Paul, and he was not completely well or completely strong.

Sometimes we are grateful for our clothes, our houses, our automobiles, or our friends. I am encouraged by my friends, and I am so very grateful for them. We should be grateful for all of these things, but that should not be the heart of the matter.

What is the real cause of gratitude? What is at the heart of the matter? The one real cause of gratitude is that our sins have been forgiven, and we are children of God. If that is a reality in your life, then that is the one thing that should be at the heart of all your gratitude. Nothing can take that away from you.

If you have asked the Lord to forgive your sin and by faith trusted Christ as your Savior, you may lose your health, but you are not going to lose your salvation. You may lose your wealth, but you are not going to lose your salvation. You may lose your house, but you are not going to lose your salvation. You may lose your capacity to function and drive an automobile and do other things, but you are not going to lose your salvation. We get so worked up about so many things that we forget the main thing. The main thing is knowing Jesus Christ as our Savior.

One evening I was walking through one of the nursing homes in our area, and I said to the man who was with me, "If we live long enough, we will be exactly like these people in this nursing home." Some could speak; some could not speak. Some could communicate intelligently; some could not. Some could walk; some could not. But the ravages of age and time were evident in every one of their lives.

Things they were grateful for had no doubt been taken away, lost long ago. But for those who are Christians, for those who have had his or her sins forgiven, something was so real that it could never be taken away.

We need to get back to believing, to understanding, to seeing through eyes of faith, that what matters most in life is knowing Jesus Christ as Savior.

We are going to have heartache in this life–sometimes a great deal of it. Every time we have a heartache, every time we have a disappointment and our life begins to sink, we need to realize that we are not grateful for what we should be truly grateful. Our gratitude should be anchored in the Lord and in the fact that our sins have been forgiven.

> *If the only reason you have for being grateful is being strong, then when you are not strong, you will not be grateful.*

THE CHARACTER OF GRATITUDE

How does gratitude behave itself? Consider our story. Christ said in Luke 17:14, *"Go shew yourselves unto the priests."* Because of the laws of Moses concerning leprosy and the cleansing of leprosy, there had to be a pronouncement of cleansing. As the leprous men were making their way, they were going by faith, believing that they had a reason to see the priest. Once they were clean, the priest had to pronounce them clean.

The Bible says, *"As they went, they were cleansed. And one of them, when he saw that he was healed,..."* Think how exciting that was. This one man *"...turned back, and with a loud voice glorified*

God." Look how the man responded. What did he do? He saw what the Lord had done for him, and he fell at the feet of the Lord Jesus and thanked Him.

Often we allow ourselves to get so carried away with all the blessings God has given us that we take our eyes off the One who has given them. This leper ran back and with a loud voice glorified God and fell on his face at the feet of the Lord Jesus and thanked Him. This is the character of gratitude. It is gratitude to God. It makes a difference in life.

We need to get back to believing, to understanding, to seeing through eyes of faith, that what matters most in life is knowing Jesus Christ as Savior.

A parent may say, "I've got children. I've worked hard to rear these kids." But people who really express the right character and gratitude do not talk this way. They talk like this: "God gave me these children and He has enabled me to be alive to work with them and try to rear them with His help and I praise Him for it." There is a definite difference in using the expression "I'm proud of you" and the expression "I'm grateful for you." The idea of gratitude begs the question–to whom are we grateful? The answer is the Lord.

All of us are so full of ourselves that we want the glory, we want the praise. But true gratitude is given to God. This is the character of gratitude.

THE CONSEQUENCES OF GRATITUDE

How does gratitude affect a person's life? How does it affect the way we live our lives? These men had been lepers. They were bound to hopeless despair because of their disease. They found company in their misery even with a Samaritan. They were on that border area of Samaria and Galilee, and this Samaritan had joined up with these leprous Jews.

The Bible says in verse seventeen, *"And Jesus answering said, Were there not ten cleansed? but where are the nine?"* If you had found the nine that did not come back, they would have said, "We are grateful." But what change did it make in their lives?

Do you know why I do what I do? Do you know why I want to be faithful to the Lord and be in the church and serve God? Because of what Christ has done for me. My life has been changed. I do not serve God "in order to" but "because of." I mean by this that I am motivated to do all I do because of what Christ has done for me. He has set me free!

The Bible says in verses eighteen and nineteen, *"There are not found that returned to give glory to God, save this stranger. And he said unto him, Arise, go thy way: thy faith hath made thee whole."* Actually by that statement, *"Thy faith hath made thee whole,"* He was saying, "Not only have you been cleansed as a leper, your lost soul is saved. You are ready, not just for time; you are ready for eternity. You are whole." God places the emphasis on the eternal.

I delight in telling you that Christ has made me whole. I am not all I should be, but I am ready for eternity. I want to do more for Christ because of what He has done for me. My last breath, if it be the next breath, will be my first breath in the presence of the Lord Jesus.

The real consequence of gratitude is that it brings a man to place the emphasis of his life on eternal things. Let us look at this from the other side. What are you emphasizing? If it is not the eternal, then you are not really grateful. When God has gotten hold of my heart about eternity, knowing that hell is real and heaven is real, that is the thing the Lord uses to speak to me.

As a Christian, eternity should have a grip upon you. The consequences of gratitude to God help us place the emphasis on eternal things. A truly grateful Christian will support God's work and be a witness for Jesus Christ. You may say the reason you do not do these things is that you do not have the money or the time; but the truth is, you do not have gratitude in your heart to God or you would be emphasizing the eternal.

Ingratitude is sin. Our lives are so brief; they are over in a moment. God said that our lives are like a vapor. The truly grateful person will place the emphasis on eternal things.

God has given us the responsibility in our churches to place the emphasis on eternity. Do you know why churches have not placed the emphasis on eternal things? It is because they are not truly grateful for what God and God alone has done. When they are, they will place the emphasis on eternal things.

I do not serve God "in order to" but "because of." I mean by this that I am motivated to do all I do because of what Christ has done for me. He has set me free!

If knowing Christ is what really matters in the end, then it should matter much more now than it does. It should matter in what we do, how we spend our time, and where we give our money. It brings about a great consequence in our lives to be truly grateful to God. The consequence is the emphasis that we place on eternity. The world is divided into groups represented by the one who came and the nine who did not return. May the Lord say of us, "[he] *turned back, and with a loud voice glorified God, and fell down on his face at his feet, giving him thanks."*

Chapter Twelve

HAVE FAITH IN GOD

 raveling in our mind's eye with the Savior those last days before Calvary, we find that Christ's triumphal entry into Jerusalem took place as our Lord was nearing the close of His earthly ministry. The people cried, *"Hosanna; Blessed is he that cometh in the name of the Lord"* (Mark 11:9). Remember that just over on the other side of the Mount of Olives were the villages of Bethphage and Bethany. Our Lord was traveling back from Bethany, up to the top of the Mount of Olives, and down the mountain across the Kedron Valley into Jerusalem. On His journey He passed a fig tree. What happened at that fig tree is something we need to have deeply implanted into our hearts.

In Mark 11:12-26 the Bible says,

> *And on the morrow, when they were come from Bethany, he was hungry: and seeing a fig tree afar off having leaves, he came, if haply he might find any thing thereon: and when he came to it, he found*

nothing but leaves; for the time of figs was not yet. And Jesus answered and said unto it, No man eat fruit of thee hereafter for ever. And his disciples heard it. And they come to Jerusalem: and Jesus went into the temple, and began to cast out them that sold and bought in the temple, and overthrew the tables of the moneychangers, and the seats of them that sold doves; and would not suffer that any man should carry any vessel through the temple. And he taught, saying unto them, Is it not written, My house shall be called of all nations the house of prayer? but ye have made it a den of thieves. And the scribes and chief priests heard it, and sought how they might destroy him: for they feared him, because all the people was astonished at his doctrine. And when even was come, he went out of the city. And in the morning, as they passed by, they saw the fig tree dried up from the roots. And Peter calling to remembrance saith unto him, Master, behold, the fig tree which thou cursedst is withered away. And Jesus answering saith unto them, Have faith in God. For verily I say unto you, That whosoever shall say unto this mountain, Be thou removed, and be thou cast into the sea; and shall not doubt in his heart, but shall believe that those things which he saith shall come to pass; he shall have whatsoever he saith. Therefore I say unto you, What things soever ye desire, when ye pray, believe that ye receive them, and ye shall have them. And when ye stand praying, forgive, if ye have ought against any: that your Father also which is in heaven may forgive you your trespasses. But if ye do not forgive, neither will your Father which is in heaven forgive your trespasses.

Notice the simple yet profound statement that Jesus Christ made to His disciples in Mark 11:22. He said, *"Have faith in God."* There is no problem we deal with and no person we encounter, no matter how difficult, that is not covered completely by this expression, *"Have faith in God."* Believe God with everything. The disciples who were following our Lord were to do His work. His work is to be done His way, and His way is the way of faith. The disciples had to learn to trust the Lord.

There is no salvation apart from faith. An intellectual attainment does not bring salvation. We are saved by the grace of God through faith. The Bible says, *"For by grace are ye saved through faith"* (Ephesians 2:8). There is no salvation apart from faith.

You can have everything intellectually in place, but there is no peace in your heart apart from faith. It is not knowledge alone that brings peace, but peace comes through faith. There is no lasting work done for God without faith.

When you and I read stories of people who have served the Lord, we are inspired by their lives. Why? What gave them the courage to do what they did? Why did they step out and attempt what they attempted? Why did these great men and women serve God and do something out of the ordinary for Him? Because they had faith in God.

I want you to see that in this passage the Lord was dealing with His disciples. Realize that these were men who were following the Lord, men who were destined to do the work of God after our Savior ascended to heaven. Above everything else, they needed to get a hold of this, *"Have faith in God."*

We cannot serve God until we do it by faith. Many men have lost the edge of the faith life by substituting the intellectual life for the faith life. Sharpen your wit, but do not substitute your wit for faith. Sharpen your mind, but do not substitute intellect for faith. I believe if God should choose one thing to equip us for life, it is what we have found here–faith in Him.

The sad story of churches and Christians that never did what they could have done always has the same commentary–it is traced to a lack of faith. *"Have faith in God."* This is a subject that should get our attention.

> We cannot serve God until we do it by faith.

If you are not a Christian, you should trust the Lord Jesus as your Savior. The object of your faith must be the Lord Jesus Christ, and you must trust Him for salvation. If you are a Christian, understand that when we reach the end of sight, we have reached the beginning of faith. Think what we can trust the Lord for. *"Have faith in God."*

THE PRODUCT OF FAITH IS FRUITFULNESS

The Bible says in Mark 11:22, *"And Jesus answering saith unto them, Have faith in God."* Notice what this statement is connected to, and you will see something very important. If we want to be fruitful, we must be faithful. Our lack of fruitfulness is directly attributed to our lack of faithfulness. The product of faith is fruitfulness.

You can read through a passage like this in the Bible and never see what is actually happening. In verse twenty-one, the Lord Jesus and His disciples were passing by the day after He had pronounced a curse on this fig tree, and it was withered from the roots.

You may go up to a tree and see death on the extreme ends of it. You may break off bits and pieces of it trying to find if there is still life. However, this fig tree in our story had withered from the roots. With this in mind, Peter made this statement in verse twenty-one, *"And Peter calling to remembrance saith unto him, Master, behold, the fig tree which thou cursedst is withered away."*

It is as though the Lord did not even make any connection to the fig tree, because the Bible says, *"And,"* connecting with verse twenty-one. *"And Jesus answering saith unto them, Have faith in God."* What was Christ trying to teach them?

Peter said, "Look at the fig tree; it's withered away," and the Lord said, *"Have faith in God."* Peter must have thought, "We are walking with the Lord; the fig tree has been cursed. It's withered away. There's nothing left, and Jesus says to have faith in God. What does He mean?"

You may think, "Well, if I've got great faith in God, I can walk around and pronounce judgment on things." The Lord was not talking about pronouncing judgment on fig trees. Christ was saying that if you do not have faith in God, you will live a withered life. Perhaps the saddest thing in life is to think of what could have been.

The product of faith is fruitfulness. Our Lord said, "If you don't want to be withered in your life and be fruitless like that fig tree, have faith in God." I do not want to be withered, and I do not want to be fruitless. Christ is the vine, and I am the branch. I want Him to be able to work through me and produce much fruit in my life.

> *The sad story of churches and Christians that never did what they could have done always has the same commentary—it is traced to a lack of faith.*

May God be able to look at us and say, "Those people have great faith." In return, others will see the fruit because the product of that faith is fruitfulness. This is the connection between the cursed, withered fig tree and the statement, *"Have faith in God."* Our Lord was saying to His disciples, "I don't want you to live withered lives. Have faith in God." The product of faith is fruitfulness.

THE PROOF OF FAITH IS WORKS

The second thing I want to show you from this passage is very simple–the proof of faith. The Bible says in Mark 11:22-23,

> *And Jesus answering saith unto them, Have faith in God. For verily I say unto you, That whosoever shall say unto this mountain, Be thou removed, and be thou cast into the sea; and shall not doubt in his heart, but shall believe that those things which he saith shall come to pass; he shall have whatsoever he saith.*

We prove our faith by our works. Please understand this, because most people attempt to operate just exactly opposite of this principle. Why do we attempt great things for God? Why do we attempt things that people say cannot be done? Because God has put something in our hearts that moves us to do it, and we are stirred and want to attempt this for God. We attempt great things for God, not knowing exactly how they are going to be brought to pass, but knowing that God has planted these things in our hearts.

> *If we want to be fruitful, we must be faithful. Our lack of fruitfulness is directly attributed to our lack of faithfulness. The product of faith is fruitfulness.*

A real Christian who is trying to live a Christian life does not look at the deed before he looks at God. He looks first at God. He may not even see the end of the deed in sight, but he just begins because God leads him to do it. It all begins with God.

If we are serving God the right way, we are serving God because we are stirred up for Him in our hearts and we want to do something for Him. We serve Him out of great faith in God. If a man believes God, he is going to do something for Him.

Can you imagine that the Lord Jesus was going to stand and tell this handful of people, *"Go ye into all the world, and preach the gospel to every creature"* (Mark 16:15)? It was an insurmountable task. It was impossible. So how did they do it? Did they have the whole plan drawn out? Did they say to the Lord, "Now this is how we're going to do it. Let us do it"? No! They started with God and said, "We're going to step out and do this by faith." Only then did God see them through. We must start with the Lord. Start with faith.

> *Christ was saying that if you do not have faith in God, you will live a withered life.*

I am a weak pile of dust, and so are you; but we have a great God. He did not say to have faith in what the people can do; He did not say to have faith in what the people can raise or in what people can sacrifice. He said, *"Have faith in God."* I cannot understand how it can be done, but I know the One who can do it. God can do it. As the children sing, "God can do anything, but fail." Have faith in God.

The Bible says in James 2:14, *"What doth it profit, my brethren, though a man say he hath faith, and have not works? can faith save him?"* In other words, faith without works is not faith. The Bible continues in James 2:15-20,

> *If a brother or sister be naked, and destitute of daily food, and one of you say unto them, Depart in peace, be ye warmed and filled; notwithstanding ye give them not those things which are needful to the body; what doth it profit? Even so faith, if it hath not works, is dead, being alone. Yea, a man may say, Thou hast faith, and I have works: shew me thy faith without*

thy works, and I will shew thee my faith by my works. Thou believest that there is one God; thou doest well: the devils also believe, and tremble. But wilt thou know, O vain man, that faith without works is dead?

The man who serves the Lord does not do something and say, "Now look. Can't you see that I'm a Christian? Look what I've done." A man who serves God for God does not do that. A man who serves God for God starts out believing God and following God. If he ever gets to stand on the other side and look back, he says, "Look what God has done."

Could it be that in every city God is looking for some people who trust Him? I believe the Savior desires to work through us to reach others. He uses those who have faith in Him.

THE EXPRESSION OF FAITH IS PRAYER

The Word of God says in Mark 11:24, *"Therefore I say unto you, What things soever ye desire, when ye pray, believe that ye receive them, and ye shall have them."* When you pray, believe.

Prayer is the expression of faith. If you could listen to people pray, you could tell one thing about their lives you could tell what kind of faith they have. Some people can pray for long periods of time but never trust God for anything. Prayer is not to become a substitute for faith. We are to pray in faith believing God for all things.

God knows if our hearts are full of faith. If we go to Him with a heart full of faith, He says it shall be done.

The world is not becoming a better place in which to live. Evil men and seducers are waxing worse and worse. The pressures around us are not getting less and less. Despite all these problems, there is a rest in faith, just like a child crawling into the lap of a parent. There is a rest in the Christian life when we by faith lay everything in the lap of God. There is a rest in faith that is found nowhere else in the world.

A miracle happened here in Mark chapter eleven. Christ and His disciples were walking, and the Lord Jesus became hungry. The Lord knew that there was no fruit on the fig tree. He was teaching His disciples something. When there was no fruit on the tree, the Bible says He cursed the tree. The next morning when they traveled that same way, Peter said, "Look, there's that same tree. It's withered from the roots."

Prayer is not to become a substitute for faith.

Jesus Christ merely said, *"Have faith in God."* If you have faith in God, you will be fruitful. If you have faith in God, what you do will prove you have faith in God. If you have faith in God, you can ask and it shall be done. Get your faith right, and the other things will fall into proper place. If we have faith, we will be bold enough to approach the throne of grace and ask our heavenly Father for what we need. Have faith in God.

Chapter Thirteen

JESUS TOUCHED HIS EAR

 s Christ was going to Calvary to bleed and die for our sins, His disciples knew that something was about to happen. When the disciples were with the Lord Jesus and news reached them about Lazarus, they talked of people seeking the life of Christ. They said, "Let's die with Him."

No doubt there was an intensity building, a feeling that something was about to happen. In the Upper Room, Judas left the presence of Christ and the other disciples. In just a few hours, there would be a meeting between Judas and the Lord Jesus.

Christ had led His disciples down the hillside, across the Kedron into the Garden of Gethsemane. It was a night of the full moon, at the time of the Passover Feast. They were praying in the garden. For the last time, Christ had gone to His disciples and awakened them from their sleep. Just as they were stirring from their sleep, the multitude arrived. Judas stepped out and betrayed Christ with a kiss.

In Matthew 26:47 the Bible says, *"And while he yet spake, lo, Judas, one of the twelve, came, and with him a great multitude with swords and staves, from the chief priests and elders of the people."*

There is a difference of opinion about how many people came to Christ in the garden. There are some interpreters of Scripture who believe that Roman soldiers were gathered with these people who came from the high priest, the temple custodians, the guards of the temple. The interpreters also believe that this group was backed up by as many as four hundred Roman soldiers. We cannot be absolutely sure of the exact details.

In two of the gospel records, the Bible does use the term *"multitude."* The Bible says in Matthew 26:48-53,

> *Now he that betrayed him gave them a sign, saying, Whomsoever I shall kiss, that same is he: hold him fast. And forthwith he came to Jesus, and said, Hail, master; and kissed him. And Jesus said unto him, Friend, wherefore art thou come? Then came they, and laid hands on Jesus, and took him. And, behold, one of them which were with Jesus stretched out his hand, and drew his sword, and struck a servant of the high priest's, and smote off his ear. Then said Jesus unto him, Put up again thy sword into his place: for all they that take the sword shall perish with the sword. Thinkest thou that I cannot now pray to my Father, and he shall presently give me more than twelve legions of angels?*

In Mark 14:43-49 the Bible says,

> *And immediately, while he yet spake, cometh Judas, one of the twelve, and with him a great multitude with swords and staves, from the chief priests and the scribes and the elders. And he that betrayed him had*

given them a token, saying, Whomsoever I shall kiss, that same is he; take him, and lead him away safely. And as soon as he was come, he goeth straightway to him, and saith, Master, master; and kissed him. And they laid their hands on him, and took him. And one of them that stood by drew a sword, and smote a servant of the high priest, and cut off his ear. And Jesus answered and said unto them, Are ye come out, as against a thief, with swords and with staves to take me? I was daily with you in the temple teaching, and ye took me not: but the scriptures must be fulfilled.

In John 18:1-3 the Bible says,

When Jesus had spoken these words, he went forth with his disciples over the brook Cedron, where was a garden, into the which he entered, and his disciples. And Judas also, which betrayed him, knew the place: for Jesus ofttimes resorted thither with his disciples. Judas then, having received a band of men and officers from the chief priests and Pharisees, cometh thither with lanterns and torches and weapons.

Since they came with all those lanterns and torches, they must have thought they were going to have to search for Christ. They may have said, "He'll be hiding somewhere. He may be somewhere in a cave. We'll need the lights to find Him." But it did not happen that way. God's Word continues in John 18:4-11,

Jesus therefore, knowing all things that should come upon him, went forth, and said unto them, Whom seek ye? They answered him, Jesus of Nazareth. Jesus saith unto them, I am he. And Judas also, which betrayed him, stood with them. As soon then as he had said unto them, I am he, they went

> *backward, and fell to the ground. Then asked he them
> again, Whom seek ye? And they said, Jesus of
> Nazareth. Jesus answered, I have told you that I am
> he: if therefore ye seek me, let these go their way: that
> the saying might be fulfilled, which he spake, Of them
> which thou gavest me have I lost none. Then Simon
> Peter having a sword drew it, and smote the high
> priest's servant, and cut off his right ear. The
> servant's name was Malchus. Then said Jesus unto
> Peter, Put up thy sword into the sheath: the cup which
> my Father hath given me, shall I not drink it?*

It is wonderful to read the parallel accounts and to see what details God gives us from one account to the other. In the Gospel according to John, the Bible gives us the name of the high priest's servant. His name was Malchus. Also, if you notice carefully, John is the only book in which Peter is named.

Before they entered into this garden scene, Christ had discussed with His disciples what things they needed to take with them. In that conversation, the subject of swords was mentioned. The Bible says that one of the disciples said, "We have two swords." Peter had one of those swords.

When I begin to think of this fisherman–a man of nets and fishing gear, robust and strong–I do not really see him with a sword strapped to his side. But he had a sword, and one of the other disciples had a sword also.

The Bible says this multitude came down the hillside in search of the Lord Jesus. Perhaps they were accompanied by Roman soldiers, clanging their way with swords and staves, carrying lanterns, moving forward and crossing the brook into Gethsemane. They must have thought they were going to have to seek out the Son of God as if hunting an animal. They were prepared for any type of skirmish they might find, reinforced by men with weapons because they suspected there may be a resistance on the part of His disciples. Because of the topography of the land, it would have been impossible not to have known they were coming.

But to their surprise, the Bible says when Christ finished praying, He went forth and met them. He stepped into their presence. Judas stepped forth and kissed Him. Never has there been a kiss as that kiss. Nothing in human history pictures such hypocrisy. The Bible tells us of two who kissed Christ. One kissed His feet in love; the other kissed His face in betrayal.

Then the Lord spoke to the multitude and said, *"Whom seek ye?"* They answered, *"Jesus of Nazareth."* He said, *"I am..."* He answered them with the same words that God gave to Moses in Exodus 3:14, *"Thus shalt thou say unto the children of Israel, I AM hath sent me unto you."*

He is more than Jesus of Nazareth. He is the eternal God. When He said, *"I am he,"* the Bible says immediately they all fell to the ground. For a moment, they were lying there on the earth, stunned in silence. They got up, and the whole thing was repeated. *"Whom seek ye? And they said, Jesus of Nazareth. Jesus answered, I have told you that I am he: if therefore ye seek me, let these go their way: that the saying might be fulfilled, which he spake, Of them which thou gavest me have I lost none."*

They began to bind His hands. At that moment, Peter could not stand the sight that he was witnessing. Here they were, binding the hands of Jesus Christ. More than likely, the high priest's servant Malchus was the one who was leading in this particular matter.

As quick as a flash, Peter drew his sword and went for the man's head. The sword glanced from Malchus' head and struck his right ear. The Bible says it severed his ear from his head.

Our Lord took the ear and reattached it to the man's head. Any facial wound bleeds profusely, and no doubt that wound was bleeding profusely. When the Lord reattached the ear, it was healed completely. This was the last miracle He performed before He went to the cross. Let us consider a few things that we understand about our Lord from this miracle.

THE POWER HE DID NOT USE

Try to picture this scene unfolding. On a number of occasions, I have gone across that brook and walked into that garden which is still preserved in the land of the Bible. I have imagined this scene unfolding. Every time I have been there, I have tried to imagine where Christ was praying and where the disciples were sleeping. I have tried to imagine, as I have looked across the Kedron up the hillside toward Jerusalem, the path that the people took who came to take Christ. Our Lord could see from a great distance that they were coming. If He had wanted to run, He could have. However, they were surprised as He stepped forth to meet them.

The Bible tells us of two who kissed Christ. One kissed His feet in love; the other kissed His face in betrayal.

When Peter drew his sword and cut off Malchus' ear, the Lord Jesus healed the man's ear. But before He healed his ear, He simply spoke and the soldiers fell to the ground. He asked Peter, *"Thinkest thou that I cannot now pray to my Father, and he shall presently give me more than twelve legions of angels?"* He had that power–power to speak and cause them to fall to the ground; power to reach down and put a man's ear back on his head and heal it; power to call twelve legions of angels.

We have a God who can do all things. God Himself asked the question to Abraham and Sarah in Genesis 18:14, *"Is any thing too hard for the LORD?"*

Consider this power that Christ had available that He did not use. Think about why He did not use it. He was on His way to the cross. He came to this earth to bleed and die for our sins. He was not taken prisoner; He yielded Himself. He was not overpowered by these men though there was a great multitude. He willingly gave His life.

As we think of this and we think of the power He did not use, we realize He did not use it because He loves us so.

THE POWER HE DID NOT NEED

As we have seen, two of Christ's disciples had swords. One of them drew his sword. If John had not told us who it was, I think we could have guessed. We would have said, "Was it the same fellow who stepped out of the boat and started walking on the water? Was it the same fellow that we read about in other places who took the lead?" But we do not have to doubt who it was. John tells us that it was Peter who took the sword and it was Malchus, the high priest's servant, who lost his ear. In this particular case, Peter pulled a sword, as if the Lord needed Peter's power to deliver Him.

There is confusion sometimes about the high priest. We read about Annas and his son-in-law Caiaphas. Annas, we are told, had been put out of power. Caiaphas had become the high priest in A.D. 18. Annas was guilty of a number of things and was no longer fit to serve as the high priest, yet he was still a man of great power. But remember that Christ was taken to Annas and then to Caiaphas.

When I was starting out as a preacher, I would preach on this story and I would give Peter a hard time. As a matter of fact, every time I would see Peter make a mistake, I would give him a hard time until

I realized that looking at Peter was like looking into a mirror and seeing myself.

We all know that God uses human instrumentality. But when we turn it around in our minds and we think that God cannot get along without us, then He allows us to see that there is a power we have that He does not need.

Peter pulling the sword was similar to Saul putting the armor on David. But if we are going to do something mighty for God, there is a certain way we are going to do it. There is a certain thing God needs from us.

Sometimes I wonder what the Lord would do without me. You may laugh, but you think the same thing. You may not say it, but you think that way. Without me, God would still be God; but without God, I am absolutely nothing.

> *Peter pulled a sword, as if the Lord needed Peter's power to deliver Him.*

If you ever get the idea that you are so big, so powerful, so able, so capable, so thoughtful, so imaginative, so administrative, such a great speaker or money maker, or so able that the Lord's work would suffer greatly if you were not around, the Lord will say to you, "Put up your sword. Compared to twelve legions of angels, what do you think that sword amounts to? I don't need your sword."

Any time we get ahead of God and try to do His work in the energy of the flesh, we are using a power that God does not need. The Lord wants to work through dead men, men who will die to self and allow the Lord to use them by working through their lives.

May God help us to humble ourselves, to seek God's face, to yield to the Lord, and allow Him to use us. But may God deliver us from thinking that He cannot get along without us.

In this instance, when Peter pulled his sword and sought to deliver the Son of God, he was out of place, blundering in the flesh. How many times have we done the same? There is a power we have that God does not need to get His work done.

THE POWER HE DID NOT DENY

In the Gospel according to John, we read also of the power that Christ did not deny. The Bible says in John 2:18, *"Then answered the Jews and said unto him, What sign shewest thou unto us, seeing that thou doest these things? Jesus answered and said unto them, Destroy this temple, and in three days I will raise it up."*

In John 10:17-18 the Bible says, *"Therefore doth my Father love me, because I lay down my life, that I might take it again. No man taketh it from me, but I lay it down of myself. I have power to lay it down, and I have power to take it again. This commandment have I received of my Father."* This is the power He would not deny.

When our Lord went forth to meet the multitude, He knew who He was and He knew why He came. He was not a trapped criminal up against the wall, trying to find a way out. It was determined by God before the world was ever created that Jesus Christ would bleed and die for our sins, be buried in a borrowed tomb, and come forth from the grave alive forevermore.

Without me, God would still be God; but without God, I am absolutely nothing.

Our Lord, calm and confident, walked right into that hour of darkness. He said, *"The hour is come."* That hour was the hour when Christ delivered Himself into the hands of sinners. He walked into it calmly and confidently because He said, *"I have power to lay it down, and I have power to take it again."* This is the God we serve.

I do not know whether Malchus ever came to Christ or not, but I imagine that there was always something thought-provoking about his right ear. The Bible says Christ touched his ear. Every time he thought about that right ear he may have thought, "I lost this thing for a moment. It was gone with a blow of a sword, severed from my head. What a night that was."

He may have said, "I can remember how we got together, how we planned and schemed, how we thought things would be, how we gathered everyone we could gather with swords and staves and torches and lanterns, and we went as a posse after Christ, this Jesus of Nazareth. I can still remember the feeling I had as I stood near the front of the crowd and He stepped forth. What a moment when He spoke and we all fell to the ground. As we were lying there, there were thoughts that ran through our minds, but we were so determined to take Him, we got up. As soon as I put my hands on His hands to bind Him, a blow came from one of His disciples. He missed my head, trying to sever my head from my shoulders, but he caught my ear and it was gone! But in a moment those same hands I was binding with ropes took that ear and put it back on my head."

I do not know whether Malchus ever got saved, but I am sure that he could not help thinking something about that ear. Has the Lord Jesus touched your life? We do not go back to a scene in Gethsemane on a moonlit night with the sword-swinging Simon Peter. But in our minds, we go somewhere where someone took an open Bible and led us to the Savior. We go somewhere where Christ stepped forth and we met Him and trusted Him as our Savior. I do not know how often Malchus thought about this ear, but we should think often about when we came to the Lord Jesus and He entered our lives.

Sunday School materials are available for use in
conjunction with *The Miracles of Jesus Volume 2.*
For a complete listing of available materials from
Crown Christian Publications, please call
1-877 AT CROWN

or write to: P.O. Box 159 ❖ Powell, TN ❖ 37849

Visit us on the Web at
FaithfortheFamily.com
"A Website for the Christian Family"

CROWN
CHRISTIAN
PUBLICATIONS
Royal Reading

ABOUT THE AUTHOR

Clarence Sexton is the pastor of the Temple Baptist Church and founder of Crown College in Knoxville, Tennessee. He has written more than twenty books and booklets. He speaks in conferences throughout the United States and has conducted training sessions for pastors and Christian workers in several countries around the world. He and his wife Evelyn have been married for thirty-seven years. They have two grown sons and six grandchildren. For more information about the ministry of Clarence Sexton, visit our website at FaithfortheFamily.com.

OTHER HELPFUL BOOKS BY CLARENCE SEXTON:

THE LORD IS MY SHEPHERD

EARNESTLY CONTEND
  FOR THE FAITH

THE CHRISTIAN HOME

TRUTHS EVERY
  CHRISTIAN NEEDS TO KNOW

LORD, SEND A REVIVAL

THE PARABLES OF JESUS
  VOLUME 1 & 2

ISSUES OF LIFE ANSWERED
  FROM THE BIBLE

THE CONCLUSION OF THE
  WHOLE MATTER VOLUME 1 & 2

THE MIRACLES OF JESUS VOLUME 1